The Behaviour Whisperer

Dealing with poor behaviour is exhausting and stressful. But it doesn't have to be! Some teachers keep their students in line with apparent ease. They defuse tricky situations with discreet words and almost imperceptible gestures. They extract work from the most reticent students. Yet even experienced teachers are not immune to the impact of bad behaviour on both the classroom environment and their own well-being. In this exciting new book, bestselling author Mark Roberts shares the secrets of how *behaviour whispering* can improve 100 common classroom problems, from the student who is *always* late to the class that is unsettled by a wasp.

Divided into two sections, Part A features 80 common behaviour scenarios that teachers are likely to encounter. Roberts reframes ineffective responses to these scenarios by using language that helps students feel supported and helps you succeed in regaining control of the situation. Part B introduces 20 non-verbal forms of communication that can be used in a variety of behaviour situations to manage the problem without singling out a troublesome or unfocused student. Each of the 100 scenarios featured in the book is accompanied by an illustration and an explanation of why this phrase or gesture works. Practical next steps follow at the end of every scenario, giving further suggestions on how to maintain good behaviour.

Providing unrivalled insight into the importance of communication and the psychology that underpins it, the book breaks behaviour down to a granular level, offering tried and trusted responses to virtually every conceivable classroom behaviour scenario at primary and secondary levels.

Mark Roberts is Director of Research at Carrickfergus Grammar School in Northern Ireland. Previously, he has worked at schools in Devon and Manchester. Mark writes books and articles about teaching and studying English and is also a frequent contributor to TES on subjects including pedagogy, behaviour, leadership and educational research.

"Like a GPS for your mouth, *The Behaviour Whisperer* helps teachers decide what to say (and what not to say) at every turn."

Peps Mccrea, *Director of Education at Steplab*

"This is an incredibly helpful and practical book, which demystifies the often complex and emotionally draining issue of classroom behaviour. Mark's key principles and classroom scenarios guide teachers at all career stages with exceptionally clear and structured advice. This is the book I wish I'd have had when I started teaching – a must-read."

Rachel Ball, *assistant principal and history teacher*

"The strategies that Mark Roberts shares in *The Behaviour Whisperer* are clear, practical and informed by a cocktail of research and hard-earned experience. Learning how to respond to the 100 common scenarios set out in this book shouldn't be a matter of trial and error, and with *The Behaviour Whisperer*, it doesn't have to be."

Jon Hutchinson, *Director of Curriculum & Teacher Development at the Reach Foundation*

"Times are changing when it comes to behaviour management. For many years, advice was freely given based on hunches and good intentions. Now, with the arrival of *The Behaviour Whisperer*, we have a beautiful blend of psychological research findings along with practical strategies. This combination of evidence-informed approach and personal experience provides a perfect formula for proactive and positive change."

Bradley Busch, *chartered psychologist and Director of InnerDrive*

"It's fair to say that, since Covid-19, behaviour has got even more challenging for teachers. For those who want to get better, it can seem like an alchemy that's almost impossible to master. Fear not! This timely, enjoyable book, packed with research, humour and concise advice will help you on your way. Written by a leader in school who is walking the walk, *The Behaviour Whisperer* doesn't promise to wave a magic wand but instead acknowledges the complexity of behaviour and acts as a book of spells teachers can keep close – a talisman to traverse the challenging terrain."

Haili Hughes, *Principal Lecturer, Director of Education, former teacher, speaker and author*

"*The Behaviour Whisperer* is the book I wished I had when I started teaching. New teachers are often thrown into the deep end and they have to deal with subtle and complex behaviour problems without the relevant tools, the relevant training or the relevant support to tackle them. This book replaces the learning around behaviour that takes years, for most teachers, through trial and error.

Mark Roberts has succinctly and comprehensively covered a range of scenarios that teachers face daily and weekly in the classroom and shown how we can deal with them without escalating a situation. Each scenario is grounded in common sense and offers tips and reasoned thinking around the choices to be made as a teacher.

Mark Roberts is the Jiminy Cricket of behaviour in the classroom, guiding us on the right path. An excellent book that guides new teachers on how to deal with behaviour and offers established teachers a new perspective on things they often take for granted. Roberts might not make you a real boy, but he will make you an even better teacher in the classroom, as far as behaviour is concerned."

Chris Curtis, *author of* How to Teach English *and head of English in a secondary school*

"In *The Behaviour Whisperer,* Mark Roberts offers essential advice for every teacher on the vital topic of behaviour management. The book is laden with practical insights based on common scenarios. It is underpinned by robust research evidence and a savvy teacher's eye. Whisper about it to every teacher you know!"

Alex Quigley, *author and National Content Manager at the Education Endowment Foundation*

"A comprehensive guide to classroom management, *The Behaviour Whisperer* serves as a practical handbook for teachers. Relatable scenarios and research-informed suggestions of how to respond in different situations make this book an invaluable addition to the school CPD library, useful to both new and experienced teachers."

Dr Jo Castelino, *assistant curriculum leader of science and homework lead*

"As I read *The Behaviour Whisperer* for the first time, I found myself experiencing something akin to the five stages of grief. I felt guilty, knowing that I had, at one time or another, mishandled each of Roberts' 100 scenarios in the early stages of my teaching career. Then I moved to a state of bewilderment, perhaps even anger, that my teaching program hadn't bothered to enlighten me with a fraction of the wisdom contained in this book. By the end, however, this book left me feeling hopeful for a profession that equips all its teachers with the skills they need to run a safe and productive classroom. As an instructional coach in a struggling school, this book is a godsend."

Zach Groshell, PhD, *instructional coach and host of the Progressively Incorrect podcast, USA*

"Mark Roberts does it again! *The Behaviour Whisperer* is the perfect addition to every teacher's bookshelf with clear strategies and micro-scripts to support with promoting effective behaviour. If you're looking to enhance your practice in the classroom, then this is just the book you need."

Yamina Bibi, *assistant headteacher, East London*

The Behaviour Whisperer

100 Ways Teachers Can Communicate to Improve Their Students' Focus in the Classroom

Mark Roberts

Routledge
Taylor & Francis Group
LONDON AND NEW YORK

Designed cover image: Caroline Tye.

First published 2025
by Routledge
4 Park Square, Milton Park, Abingdon, Oxon OX14 4RN

and by Routledge
605 Third Avenue, New York, NY 10158

Routledge is an imprint of the Taylor & Francis Group, an informa business

British Library Cataloguing-in-Publication Data
A catalogue record for this book is available from the British Library

ISBN: 978-1-032-57753-1 (hbk)
ISBN: 978-1-032-57752-4 (pbk)
ISBN: 978-1-003-44082-6 (ebk)

DOI: 10.4324/9781003440826

Typeset in Melior
by KnowledgeWorks Global Ltd.

Printed and bound in Great Britain by Bell & Bain Ltd, Glasgow

This book is dedicated to the memory of Joan Christie CVO OBE (1945–2023).

Contents

Glossary

ADHD Attention-deficit/hyperactivity disorder. Symptoms of ADHD include inattention, hyperactivity and impulsivity.

Cognitive load First researched by Sweller (1998), cognitive load theory considers the limited amount of information our working memory can cope with at one time. When cognitive load is too great, we struggle to complete tasks successfully.

Cold call Developed by Lemov (2010), cold calling is a questioning strategy where rather than asking for a volunteer, the teacher poses a question and calls on a specific student to respond.

Deliberate practice A term used by Ericsson (1993) to describe practice that "is a highly structured activity, the explicit goal of which is to improve performance. Specific tasks are invented to overcome weaknesses, and performance is carefully monitored to provide cues for ways to improve it further."

Do now tasks Brief starter activities that get students focused as soon as they enter the classroom. As part of a routine, students do not require instructions from the teacher to begin.

Front loading Front loading involves giving students precise instructions of what the task requires and what is expected of them before the teacher gets them started on a task.

Narrating the positives Rather than looking around the classroom and rebuking misbehaving students, narrating the positives involves recognising good behaviour instead. This encourages students who aren't following expectations to modify their behaviour so that they all receive positive acknowledgment.

Poor proxies for learning Coe (2015) identified things that students do that can lead us to incorrectly assume that learning is taking place, such as students appearing busy and engaged in tasks.

PPA Planning, preparation and assessment time in UK schools. Statutory non-contact time away from students during a teacher's timetabled week.

Retrieval practice Recalling knowledge from memory to improve learning. Retrieving something from your memory in a low-stakes environment increases the chance of being able to recall it in future.

Seat work A term used by educators in the United States to describe work done by students at their desks in a classroom.

Self-concept How we think about and perceive ourselves. This view is vital as it influences our motivations, attitudes and behaviours.

Self-efficacy Introduced by Bandura (1977), self-efficacy is a person's belief in their ability to succeed in a particular situation.

SEND Special educational needs and disabilities. A learning difficulty and/or a disability, where students need special health and education support.

SLT In the UK, the senior leadership team. Will vary in number and size depending on the type of school but will typically include headteacher, deputy and assistant headteachers.

Think/pair/share An activity where students are asked a question, given the opportunity to consider possible responses individually, then discuss with a partner before settling on a final answer.

Wait time The amount of time given by a teacher before students are expected to answer a question. Teachers often expect quick responses, but students benefit from a longer wait time.

Introduction

Teaching is a difficult endeavour. Getting a large, diverse group of children or young people to learn things is hard enough. Other factors – like the classroom environment, group dynamics, timetabling issues – can make a challenging job even more challenging.

Research confirms what those of us in the profession already know: teaching is a stressful job[1]. As Taxer et al.[2] highlight, teachers are more vulnerable to emotional exhaustion – a key symptom of burnout – than workers in many other occupations[3]. And what causes teachers' emotional exhaustion? The research picture frequently identifies two key culprits: excessive workload and poor student behaviour[4]. And to have a damaging impact on teachers, negative behaviour doesn't have to be extreme. As Clunies-Ross et al. make clear, "even minor disruptive behaviours have been shown to sap teachers' energy, cause teacher stress and increase the likelihood of burnout'[5]. Low-level disruption is draining.

The behaviour problem

That classroom discipline issues contribute heavily towards emotional exhaustion will not surprise teachers. Indeed, if you speak to teachers about student behaviour, many will tell you that, post-Covid, it's getting worse.

Research confirms these anecdotal beliefs. A 2023 survey conducted by Kapow found that 80% of primary teachers believed behaviour had deteriorated over the past couple of years[6]. A recent poll by Teacher Tapp, an organisation that surveys over 10,000 teachers each day, found that 37% of teachers felt that learning "largely stopped due to poor behaviour in the last lesson they taught"[7]. Furthermore, a 2022 report by the Gatsby Foundation found that "two-thirds of teachers said their displeasure was caused by behavioural issues." The report highlighted that for inexperienced secondary school teachers "student behaviour rather than subject knowledge is at the root of the problem in their least enjoyable classes, with over 80% naming it as an issue"[8]. Very experienced teachers are not immune, however, from the impact of poor behaviour: "26% of teachers with

DOI: 10.4324/9781003440826-1

more than twenty years' service" faced serious disruption in their most recently taught lesson[9].

What's more, the evidence suggests that poor behaviour is contagious and that witnessing "other students misbehaving makes it much more likely that students will misbehave themselves"[10]. Given that poor behaviour begets further disruption and has a negative impact on student attainment[11], it's little wonder that teachers feel worn out and stressed dealing with it.

Why do so many teachers struggle with behaviour?

Very little of my teacher training course was dedicated to behaviour management. Instead, we were expected to learn on the job. This often involved sink or swim situations with challenging classes that could smell the blood of inexperience in the deep waters of the classroom. Some of us were lucky enough to receive excellent advice from mentors. Others received unhelpful tips or were left to try and work it out on our own.

Research indicates that teachers often feel unequipped to deal with misbehaviour. As Moore et al. state, "teachers often lack the knowledge or training to implement effective classroom management strategies reducing problem behaviour responses"[12]. Thompson and Webber (2010) concur, arguing that:

> Teachers frequently identify classroom behaviour management as an area in which they would like to receive more training. Most preservice teacher training programs fail to equip teachers with basic methods of positive classroom reinforcement... Therefore more effective and feasible strategies for classroom management of difficult students should be provided to teachers who are already in teaching positions.[13]

If they're lucky, teachers get to pick up some pointers from expert colleagues. Otherwise, they must learn the hard way, through mortifying mistakes. We know from research around effective teaching, however, that leaving someone to discover how to do something for themselves is an ineffective and inefficient strategy. Especially when it is something as challenging as managing the behaviour of a class of 30 students. Some teachers eventually find a way, but others leave the profession or view poor behaviour as something they must simply endure throughout their career.

It's unsurprising then, that when asked "if they could wave a magic wand" and suddenly get better at one area of their teaching, 23% of respondents (the largest percentage for any category) wished to be more proficient at behaviour management[14].

The behaviour whisperers

Unfortunately, unless they work in schools of witchcraft and wizardry, teachers are unable to get their hands on magic wands. Yet some teachers can keep their students in line, despite no trickery being involved. With apparent ease, using discreet words and subtle gestures, they defuse difficult situations. These same teachers squeeze work out of the most reticent students. Somehow, they shift students' negative attitudes and motivate them to strive for success. How do they achieve this? What are the secrets of this apparent sorcery?

These teachers are behaviour whisperers. Through their skilful communication, they can settle unruly pupils. Through their understanding of human psychology, they can put the most stubborn and begrudging learners on the right path.

The Behaviour Whisperer is designed for both primary and secondary teachers. While some of the scenarios are more likely to occur with older children, there's a growing sense that issues that would traditionally be faced by secondary teachers are now emerging earlier.

Whether you teach eight-year-olds or teenagers, by using the strategies in this book, you'll be adopting the methods of the behaviour whisperers. Over time, you should find that your students become more reasonable, more responsive and more driven. Like a horse whisperer calming a headstrong stallion, you'll be able to talk to students in a way that will increase compliance and motivate them to learn. You'll know the best communication techniques for the plethora of challenging situations that you'll face in the classroom. Whether you're a trainee teacher or a hardened veteran, this book will give you a tried and tested line, or gesture, for every scenario.

How do behaviour whisperers manage behaviour so well?

This book includes 100 scenarios that will help you with all aspects of behaviour management. But before we turn to the classroom scenarios, let us first consider the ten key principles of behaviour whispering. Apply these ideas in the scenarios that follow and you'll find that dealing with problematic behaviour begins to feel much less daunting.

Set clear expectations

We've established that expecting teachers to work out how to manage behaviour for themselves is unfair. The same goes, Murphy and Van Brunt assert, for students and expectations of their behaviour:

> Expecting students to behave a certain way in the classroom without clearly delineating these expectations is like giving them a test they didn't have a chance to study for ahead of time.[15]

We need to make obvious what we expect of students. If we fail to do so, students will make assumptions about the kind of behaviour that is expected in our classroom. As Iaconelli and Anderman point out, "whether communicated through intentional or unintentional means, all teachers set expectations and goals for their students"[16]. In other words, when we don't provide explicit expectations of desired classroom behaviour students fill this vacuum of uncertainty. They do this by guessing what we permit based on what we *don't* say, rather than what we *do* say. This can lead to a disconnect between the behaviour we hope to see and the behaviour we actually see.

By contrast, given clear expectations students are far more likely to go along with them, even if they have rebellious inclinations. While some children are prone to challenging a teacher's authority, they will generally acquiesce to rules that are fair, reasonable, justified and consistently applied[17].

Reinforce classroom norms

Clear expectations are very necessary but not sufficient. In addition to setting clear boundaries, we need to revisit these expectations frequently, highlighting and modelling them constantly and reinforcing them consistently over time.

Seeing poor behaviour encourages other students to behave poorly. When teachers don't address unwanted behaviours, students interpret this as an unspoken sign that classroom expectations don't really matter. When teachers ignore violations of classroom rules, Segrist et al. note, "students will quickly learn that the informal norms are more powerful than the formal rules"[18]. Put simply, turning a blind eye to students talking over you, for example, encourages other students to also talk over you, despite the presence of a laminated sign on the wall forbidding talking over the teacher.

For this reason, how we address poor behaviour is of particular importance. When uncivil behaviour occurs, addressing it effectively helps to stem the flow of disruption. Reminders about unacceptable conduct, like low-level chatter or wondering around the classroom, prevent outbreaks of further disruption, as they stop other students from imitating the poor conduct[19]. When delivered in a measured manner, which doesn't shame or humiliate students, reminders about expectations demonstrate 'that everyone has a part of maintaining a positive and orderly classroom environment; it is not just the teacher's responsibility'[20]. Reinforcing behaviour norms ensures that good behaviour becomes a collective enterprise.

Create a sense of belonging

When students feel a sense of belonging in school they have better behaviour, motivation and attainment[21]. But what exactly do we mean by belonging in an educational context? For Goodenow (1993a), belonging in schools can be defined as:

> students' sense of being accepted, valued, included and encouraged by others (teacher and peers) in the academic classroom setting and of feeling oneself to be an important part of the life and activity of the class.[22]

Feeling like you fit in can be yourself and are respected by your teacher and classmates contributes significantly to self-esteem and strongly influences behaviour[23]. In simple terms, creating an environment where students feel valued, and part of a unified group, improves behaviour.

So how should teachers create a sense of belonging? Well, the expectations and norms we've just covered are an important place to start. According to Kiefer et al. (2015), feelings of belonging and mutual respect are generated by teachers "modelling respectful behaviour, explicitly stating classroom norms, and encouraging students to interact respectfully"[24].

A second essential component of developing student belonging is effective communication. Behaviour whisperers use language with extreme care, choosing phrases that instil clear boundaries but with a tone that ensures students feel valued and part of a close-knit group. For example, teachers who learn students' names quickly, and have make time for conversations with students before and after class, give students a stronger sense of affinity[25]. Furthermore, when discussing expectations, they're more likely to use the pronoun "we" than the pronoun "you" to foster a strong sense of inclusivity and collective aims:

> words such as 'we' can promote solidarity between teachers and students and help to promote a cooperative atmosphere in the classroom where teachers and students work together on a common goal.[26]

Language that implies that teachers and students have a unified goal increases feelings of belonging and improves behaviour.

Be firm but caring

When it comes to behaviour management, Walker (2009) identifies three different teaching styles: authoritarian, authoritative and permissive. Authoritarian teachers set strict behaviour guidelines and place little emphasis on nurturing their students. Authoritative teachers also have high expectations of classroom conduct but spend considerable time nurturing their students, ensuring they feel valued and respected. Permissive teachers display low control over student behaviour and place moderate emphasis on student nurture. Given the research on belonging, you'll be unsurprised to read that:

> the best student outcomes were associated with an authoritative teaching style. Students in this classroom were confident, engaged, and made significant year-end achievement gains.[27]

If you want to have students who are motivated, well-behaved and successful, an authoritative teaching style is key. Adopting a more permissive style leads to a chaotic classroom environment. An authoritarian style, by contrast, may ensure an orderly classroom but usually leads to feelings of resentment and demotivates students, meaning they're less likely to work hard.

Authoritarian teachers, who often rely on threatening language to control a class, can struggle to maintain good behaviour over time. A 2023 study by García-Rodríguez et al. cites findings from longitudinal research where "relationships with teachers that are primarily high in conflict or low in closeness are significantly related to behavioural problems observed in later moments"[28]. Shouting, pressure-inducing language and coercion might work to control behaviour in the short-term. But to maintain positive relationships with students over the long-term, you need to set very clear boundaries while also showing you care about them as individuals.

Stay calm and tackle issues discreetly

What makes teachers angry? Research frequently pinpoints classroom disruption as the number one trigger[29]. Often, the accumulation of "low-level" disruption leads to outbursts of anger that appears to come from nowhere but is, in reality, provoked by the stress of dealing with constant interruptions. Indeed, a Teacher Tapp survey from October 2022 found that "teachers who had learning stop completely at some point [during their last lesson] were more likely to have lost their temper in a disproportionate way"[30].

While anger is an understandable response to consistently poor behaviour, it has damaging repercussions. Reid et al. (2010), for example, found that shouting was seen by pupils as ineffective and harmful to long-term teacher student relationships[31]. A more recent study by Kaufmann found that when students view a teacher's communication as confrontational, "they are more likely to report that the learning environment is unhelpful, not conducive to their welfare, unhealthy and not engaging". Specifically, in this combative environment, students felt unable or unwilling to share opinions and contribute ideas[32].

A classic study by McPherson et al. found that when feelings of anger are expressed in a confrontational way (for example yelling and threatening) or in a passive-aggressive manner (such as making sarcastic comments), students perceive the teacher's communication as unacceptable. By stark contrast, McPherson et al. illustrate how direct but non-threatening language is the only communication style that is seen by students as reasonable and likely to improve their behaviour. As such, McPherson et al. advise that:

> Teachers should avoid intense, aggressive anger displays, and instead assertively discuss the problem with the class, try to be fair and open, and take into account students' reactions.[33]

Sarcasm seems to be particularly unpopular with students. Wanzer et al. found that students dislike humour that targets individual students, whether intended to cause upset or not[34]. Students' aversion to teacher sarcasm is perhaps best explained by the sense that the power dynamic is skewed. Where teachers use sardonic humour to belittle misbehaving students, it is viewed, unsurprisingly, as an abuse of authority[35]. For this reason, no matter how infuriated you feel, avoid sarcastic responses at all costs.

As well as avoiding aggressive or sarcastic methods, it's also very important to manage behaviour as discreetly as possible. Infantino and Little (2005) found that 78% of students felt that private reprimands were most effective when tackling inappropriate behaviour[36]. Only 12% felt that a public telling off was the most effective. Other studies have similar findings: students are least incentivised to modify their behaviour when subjected to some form of public embarrassment[37]. For students who seek peer approval by displaying rebellious, anti-school attitudes, public rebukes can make things worse. As Infantino and Little observe, students "are more likely to act inappropriately and engage in troublesome behaviour if they know that they are going to receive social rewards from peers when they are reprimanded loudly"[38]. By telling students off in a more discreet manner, you can avoid advertising their negative behaviours to the rest of the class.

De-escalate problem situations

As we have seen, when teachers respond to poor behaviour in a confrontational manner, relationships can deteriorate further. Research indicates that aggressive responses to poor behaviour, like yelling at students, lead to worsening behaviour. Lewis (2001) found that belligerent reactions to poor student conduct were "related to higher levels of student disruption and of misbehaviour"[39]. A later study by Dilekmen (2011) concurred, finding that:

> Negative approaches adopted by teachers in the management of undesired student behaviours led to an increase rather than a decrease in the problematic behaviours of the students.[40]

Staying calm when faced with minor but repeated disruption is essential. Although it is far from easy, the same approach is required when having to contend with more serious incidents. Indeed, Murphy and Van Brunt argue that:

> Teachers need skills in crisis de-escalation to offer effective intervention for disruptive or dangerous behaviour. These skills include adopting a stance of equanimity in the face of chaos or crisis; avoiding shaming or embarrassing the student; staying solution-focused (that is, addressing the immediate crisis and leaving larger corrective actions for a later time).[41]

But teachers don't receive crisis management training. Instead, it is assumed, unfairly, that they will pick up crisis management skills as they go. As a result, they are left to flounder and face the harsh consequences of their errors. Some will learn the hard way. Others will never quite manage to display that "stance of equanimity in the face of crisis". Using the scenarios in this book, I'm hoping to show you how to avoid making some of the mistakes I've made. I'm hoping to outline strategies that are useful in a crisis. I'm hoping to give you authoritative but calming stock phrases that help to improve the situation rather than make it worse.

Adopt proactive strategies

Crisis de-escalation is a vital component of behaviour management. But, often, these crises are avoidable. With a proactive approach to behaviour, it's possible to identify and nullify prospective issues before they snowball into significant problems.

By spotting poor behaviour at an early stage (before, or as it begins to occur), and communicating in a calm and direct manner, teachers can snuff out misbehaviour that could become much more serious. Yet research suggests that teachers tend to wait until problems occur before tackling them:

> Studies have shown that the predominant teacher response to disruptive student behaviour is reactive and punitive rather than proactive and positive. The reactive approach does little to decrease disruptive student behaviour.[42]

Proactive strategies can help to avoid angry responses to misbehaviour. Furthermore, because they stop small behaviour issues mushrooming into something big, proactive strategies also do wonders for teachers' blood pressure. Clunies-Ross et al. conclude that "the use of predominantly reactive management strategies has a significant relationship with elevated teacher stress and decreased student on-task behaviour"[43]. In other words, when we wait for poor behaviour to happen before addressing it, we face increased stress levels and greater disruption. When we intervene earlier, using direct but non-confrontational methods, we reduce our stress levels and have fewer serious behaviour issues to deal with.

Increase your use of non-verbal communication

Gestures are a fundamental form of communication. Classic research like Hall et al. (1977) shows that:

> The mediating mechanism [between teacher expectations and pupil behaviour] is some kind of nonverbal communication. These behaviours, not the teacher's belief per se, are what bring about changes in the pupil's behaviour.[44]

Put another way, the gestures we use appear to have an even greater influence on improving students' behaviour than spelling out our expectations. Indeed, some researchers go as far as arguing that "most interpersonal communication is non-verbal"[45]. Our body language and facial expressions, whether intentional or otherwise, have a massive influence on our relationships with students.

Yet, in my experience, most teachers fail to take advantage of non-verbal communication when managing behaviour. Research by Zeki (2009) supports my anecdotal hunch, arguing that "teachers often forget about or underestimate the importance of non-verbal communication"[46]. So, gestures are a) very important and b) often underused.

But what are the specific benefits of non-verbal communication when managing behaviour?

The first is practical. Teaching involves what physicians call "high occupational voice demands". Research indicates that "the majority of teachers have experienced vocal problems and 5% suffer from problems so severe that their working ability is questionable"[47]. The gestures in the second section of this book, therefore, provide an ideal opportunity to rest your battered vocal chords.

The second reason is cognitive. Using gestures to correct undesirable behaviour helps to maintain the attention of the rest of the class:

> When teachers use a public verbal reminder to a student who is talking or not paying attention, it disrupts other students from the flow of the lesson...[48]

From a learning perspective, interruptions – including the teacher stopping to tell students off – leave a "wake", whereby students struggle to regain focus after a disruption[49]. As such, keeping these interruptions to a minimum is vital. Gestures are crucial in keeping the class focused while teachers deal with individual misbehaviour.

Third, as Dhaem (2012) reminds us, verbal reprimands "may give inappropriate attention to the student"[50]. In a situation where students seek attention or social kudos through poor behaviour, it is critical that teachers don't unintentionally reward the student by constantly drawing attention to the poor behaviour. By their wordless nature, gestures rob some students of the negative limelight they crave.

Fourth, most non-verbal signals can disguise teacher's anger and frustration. Minus a tone of confrontation, gestures help keep good order without damaging teacher-student relationships.

The study by Dhaem found that when teachers were given training on using non-verbals to manage behaviour, participants noticed the difference, with 79% of teachers stating that they went on to use gestures more frequently. And the impact on their teaching?

> The majority of participants reported that they felt they had better classroom control and over 80% cited nonverbal hints as the strategy they use most frequently[51].

Using the non-verbal signals from Part B of the book should also help improve your control of the classroom.

Avoid overpraising

As we've seen previously, public rebukes can be counterproductive. Generally, telling students off discreetly generates better behaviour. The same can also be said for praise. The aforementioned Infantino and Little study found that students "prefer being praised quietly for good work and good behaviour"[52]. Houghton et al. had similar findings, explaining that students felt that private praise was "less embarrassing" than public compliments as it didn't "single out the student and make their behaviour noticeable to others"[53]. Indeed, research by Burnett revealed that students often worry that public praise might lead to "negative social consequences including bullying, teasing and belittlement"[54].

Empty praise can also damage students' academic self-belief. Stipek (2010) exposes how:

> Praise for successful performance on an easy task can be interpreted by a student as evidence that the teacher has a low perception of his or her ability. As a consequence, it can actually lower rather than enhance self-confidence.[55]

Put simply, in an effort to improve behaviour, some teachers lavish praise on students for the most basic stuff. Well done for writing down the title! 2 + 2 does equal 4, excellent! Yet rather than boosting students' confidence in their abilities, students pick up on the empty nature of the praise, interpreting it instead as a sign of our low expectations of their academic potential.

An interesting question is: what happens in classrooms where students behave well and work hard in lessons but don't receive regular praise? Well, research by Skipper and Douglas (2015) found that experiences of success alone are enough to "help children develop and maintain a positive relationship with their teacher"[56].

To praise or not to praise? The choice is yours. But if you do wish to use praise to try and motivate students to work hard, ensure that the praise is a) fully justified and b) delivered subtly.

Make reasonable adjustments

All students learn better in a calm and orderly environment. And all students need clear boundaries and consistent expectations. Yet some students require reasonable adjustments to ensure their specific needs are met. The key word here is specific. It's vital that you don't treat SEND students as a homogenous mass, making assumptions about how they will behave based on a label. Getting to know SEND students, as well as the contents of their individual plans, is vital.

For example, some neurodivergent students, especially those on the autism spectrum, may feel uncomfortable maintaining eye contact or may struggle to interpret your non-verbal signals. Dhaem (2010) suggests that where students fail to grasp the meaning of gestures, you might "instead silently give the student a note saying 'I want you to stop talking while other people are talking'"[57].

Avoiding prolonged eye contact with certain students is something that the vast majority of teachers are happy to accommodate. But what about asking teachers to change their approach to students who fidget during lessons? If we were to list the behaviours that frustrate teachers most, fidgeting would probably feature quite prominently. But what if I told you that, increasingly, research indicates that fidgeting – for example, movements such as leg tapping or pen clicking – has a functional cognitive role, which can actually help students focus[58]. Doodling, for example, can help students maintain attention. Andrade (2009) compared the performance of two groups that had to listen to a dull and long-winded message, finding that:

> The doodling group performed better on the monitoring task and recalled 29% more information on a surprise memory test. Unlike many dual task situations, doodling while working can be beneficial.[59]

A later study by Tadayon and Afhami (2016) found similar cognitive benefits for doodlers[60]. So how can we explain apparent functional advantages for an activity that teachers instinctively view as disruptive?

As clinical psychologist and ADHD specialist Roland Rotz explains, fidgeting is:

> our body's way of self-regulating. At times when we're under focused, or having a hard time concentrating, this is the body's natural way of stimulating itself. And the interesting thing is that it shows up so much more in ADHD folks but it's certainly true for just about anyone.[61]

Neuroscientist Anne Churchland concurs, arguing that during fidgeting "movements activate the very cognitive machinery that we need to do a difficult task"[62]. Put simply, when we're struggling to concentrate, fidgeting can nudge us towards the focus zone, especially if we have ADHD. For this reason, teachers should be wary of displaying annoyance as soon as they witness students fidgeting. As science writer Dr Kat Arney notes:

> Rather than being seen as a symptom of a lack of concentration that needs to be suppressed, fidgeting helps many people focus, relax and tackle tasks more effectively.[63]

Unaware of the potential benefits of fidgeting, most teachers will display dissatisfaction when students wriggle in their seats or doodle while working. Anne Churchland notes that noticeable fidgeters, whether adults or children, are often viewed disapprovingly by others:

People are paying a big social cost for these movements and yet they persist in doing them. And that's what got me thinking that these movements must be serving some function.[64]

In other words, the fact that heavy fidgeters annoy their teachers, workmates and family members but continue to fidget reinforces Churchland's belief that fidgeting carries cognitive benefits. Otherwise, to appease others, fidgeters would be more likely to stop their movements. Instead, fidgeters continue to use movement to kickstart their focus regardless of the opprobrium they face.

Given this knowledge, should we offer active encouragement to students, prompting them to fidget rather than attempting to suppress their movements?

Well, according to Roland Rotz, the answer is not that straightforward. Because fidgeting to gain focus is a delicate balancing act. As Rotz explains, intricate doodles or fancy fiddle toys can cause distraction rather than help us to stay in the attention zone:

Sometimes that doodle becomes more interesting than the lecture. And that's when we know that the fidget is not really working as a tool. It should operate in the background, but it becomes foreground.[65]

Take a student drawing a picture of the Eiffel Tower, for example. Rotz explains how research shows that an elaborate doodle like an illustration of a famous building is far less effective at helping students gain focus than something simple, like shading in a box or circle. The reason for this is that complicated drawings require a range of focus-sapping artistic skills, while shading in is just a "subtle, rapid, rhythmic motor movement"[66].

If we find, therefore, that students are fidgeting for a short time to help them refocus, we should allow these brief periods of fidgeting. But if the fidgeting begins to distract them from the task at hand, then we should discreetly guide them towards less intrusive fidget strategies.

Nothing illustrates how fidgeting can sometimes lead to distraction better than the disastrous fidget spinner craze of the late-2010s. Rotz describes a problem that teachers from that period recognise well: "fidget spinners are a fidget toy, very attractive and fun to look at, but not a good tool". Rotz's distinction between "toy" and "tool" is key here. A toy works as a diversion, an entertaining gadget for a bored child. But in the classroom, this toy creates a significant distraction. Indeed, crucially, flashy fidget toys don't just distract the student using them; they also distract other students in the class. For this reason, Rotz insists, fidgets should only use an unobtrusive classroom tool, "operated as a motor event that doesn't require watching it or seeing it"[67].

Reasonable adjustments for an individual child must, therefore, also consider other children. While pen tapping might help one child focus, it will disrupt the learning of the rest of the class. As you'll see from the scenarios involving fidgeting, it's possible to respect the needs of certain students while not wrecking the concentration of others.

Using this book

The 100 scenarios in this book are based on situations I've experienced or witnessed during 16 years of teaching. Some of the scenarios will occur frequently, while others will hopefully happen very rarely. Busy teachers who require help with behaviour can dip in and out of this book as issues arise. Or if they prefer, they can move through the scenarios sequentially.

Reading the book, you might feel that in places the advice seems repetitive. This is deliberate on my part. In the same way that students need repeated reminders of behaviour expectations, you'll also benefit from repeated reminders of effective communication.

Over time, these little scripts should develop your classroom communication to ensure better behaviour. The list of scenarios, however, although lengthy, won't be exhaustive. Inevitably, I will have overlooked some possible scenarios. Where this happens, you should still be able to use the principles and similar scenarios to formulate a useful response. As you become a behaviour whisperer, you'll have the skills to address most situations. But as a behaviour whisperer, you'll also find that, gradually, you have fewer situations to manage.

Notes

1 Johnson, S., Cooper, C., Cartwright, S., Donald, I., Taylor, P., & Millet, C. (2005) 'The experience of work-related stress across occupations', *Journal of Managerial Psychology*, 20:2, pp. 178–187.

2 Taxer, J.L., Becker-Kurz, B., & Frenzel, A.C. (2019) 'Do quality teacher–student relationships protect teachers from emotional exhaustion? The mediating role of enjoyment and anger', *Social Psychology of Education*, 22, pp. 209–226.

3 de Heus, P., & Diekstra, R.F.W. (1999) 'Do teachers burn out more easily? A comparison of teachers with other social professions on work stress and burnout symptoms', in R. Vandenberghe & A.M. Huberman (Eds.), *Understanding and Preventing Teacher Burnout: A Sourcebook of International Research and Practice* (pp. 269–284), New York: Cambridge University Press.

4 See, for example, Hakanen, J.J., Bakker, A.B., & Schaufeli, W.B. (2006) 'Burnout and work engagement among teachers', *Journal of School Psychology*, 43:6, pp. 495–513; Jacobson, D. (2016) 'Causes and Effects of Teacher Burnout', *Walden University Scholar Works*, pp. 1-160 and Haberman, (2004) 'Teacher burnout in Black and White'. Retrieved 29 June 2023 from https://habermanfoundation.org/teacher-burnout-in-black-and-white/

5 Clunies-Ross, P., Little, E., & Kienhuis, M. (2008) 'Self-reported and actual use of proactive and reactive classroom management strategies and their relationship with teacher stress and student behaviour', *Educational Psychology*, 28, pp. 693–710.

6 Kapow Primary (2023) 'How did the Covid pandemic impact primary school children's attention?', 13 June 2023, available at: https://www.kapowprimary.com/blog/how-did-the-covid-pandemic-impact-primary-school-childrens-attention-spans/

7 Teacher Tapp (2023) 'Coronation themed lessons, school behaviour and marking', 10 May 2023, available at: https://teachertapp.co.uk/articles/coronation-themed-lessons-school-behaviour-and-marking/

8 Allen, B., Ford, I., & Hannay, T. (2022) 'Teacher Recruitment, Job Attachment and Career Intentions after the COVID-19 Pandemic', Gatsby Foundation Report, available at: https://www.gatsby.org.uk/uploads/education/220620-teacher-recruitment-teacher-tapp-schooldash-gatsby-final.pdf

9 Teacher Tapp (2022) 'Installing updates, behaviour, GCSEs and how many emails?!', 17 October 2002, available at: https://teachertapp.co.uk/articles/installing-updates-behaviour-gcses-how-many-emails/

10 Segrist, D., Bartels, L. K. and Nordstrom, C. R, (2018) '"But Everyone Else is Doing It:" A Social Norms Perspective on Classroom Incivility', *College Teaching*, 66:4, pp. 181–186.

11 Little, E., & Hudson, A. (1998) 'Conduct problems and treatment across home and school: a review of the literature', *Behaviour Change*, 14, pp. 213–227.

12 Moore, T. C., Wehby, J. H., Oliver, R. M., Chow, J. C., Gordon, J. R., & Mahany, L. A. (2017) 'Teachers' Reported Knowledge and Implementation of Research-Based Classroom and Behaviour Management Strategies', *Remedial and Special Education*, 38:4, pp. 222–232.

13 Thompson, A. M., & Webber, K. C. (2010) 'Realigning student and teacher perceptions of school rules: A behaviour management strategy for students with challenging behaviours', *Children & Schools*, 32:2, pp. 71–79 citing Maag, J. (2001) 'Rewarded by Punishment: Reflections on the Disuse of Positive Reinforcement in Education', *Exceptional Children*, 67, pp. 173–186.

14 Teacher Tapp (2023) 'Coronation themed lessons, school behaviour and marking', 10 May 2023, available at: https://teachertapp.co.uk/articles/coronation-themed-lessons-school-behaviour-and-marking/

15 Murphy, A., & Van Brunt, B. (2018) 'Addressing dangerous behaviour in the classroom: A three-pronged approach can help educators prevent or de-escalate classroom crises', *Educational Leadership*, 76:1, p. 66–70.

16 Iaconelli, R., & Anderman, E.M. (2021) 'Classroom goal structures and communication style: the role of teacher immediacy and relevance-making in students' perceptions of the classroom', *Social Psychology of* Education, 24:1, pp. 37–58.

17 See, for example, Deutsch, N. L. (2005) '"I like to treat others as others treat me": The development of prosocial selves in an urban youth organisation', In D. B. Fink (issue editor) & G. G. Noam (editor-in-chief), *Doing the Right Thing: Ethical development across diverse environments. New directions for youth development.* (108, pp. 89–106). San Francisco: Jossey Bass.
Smetana, J. G., & Turiel, E. (2003) 'Moral development during adolescence', In G. R. Adams & M. D. Berzonsky (Eds.), *Blackwell handbook of adolescence* (pp. 247–268), Malden, MA: Blackwell.

18 Segrist, D., Bartels, L. K. and Nordstrom, C. R, (2018) '"But Everyone Else is Doing It:" A Social Norms Perspective on Classroom Incivility', *College Teaching*, 66:4, pp. 181–186.

19 Baker, K. (1985) 'Research evidence of a school discipline problem', *Phi Delta Kappan*, 66, pp. 482–488.

20 Dhaem, J. (2012) 'Responding to Minor Misbehaviour through Verbal and Nonverbal Responses', *Beyond Behaviour*, 21:3, pp. 29–34.

21 H. Korpershoek, E. T. Canrinus, M. Fokkens-Bruinsma & H. de Boer (2020) 'The relationships between school belonging and students' motivational, social-emotional, behavioural, and academic outcomes in secondary education: a meta-analytic review', *Research Papers in Education*, 35:6, pp. 641–680.

22 Goodenow, C. (1993a) 'Classroom belonging among early adolescents students' relationships to motivation and achievement', *Journal of Early Adolescence*, 13:1, pp. 21–40.

23 Pittman, L. D., & Richmond, A. (2007) 'Academic and psychological functioning in late adolescence: The importance of school belonging', *Journal of Experimental Education*,

75, pp. 270–290 and Wilson, D., Jones, D., Bocell, F., Crawford, J., Kim, M. J., Veilleux, N., Floyd-Smith, T., Bates, R., & Plett, M. (2015) 'Belonging and academic engagement among undergraduate STEM students: A multi-institutional study', *Research in Higher Education*, 56:7, pp. 750–776.

24 Kiefer, S. M., Alley, K. M., & Ellerbrock, C. R. (2015) 'Teacher and Peer Support for Young Adolescents' Motivation, Engagement, and School Belonging', *RMLE Online*, 38:8, pp. 1–18.

25 Iaconelli, R., & Anderman, E.M. (2021) 'Classroom goal structures and communication style: the role of teacher immediacy and relevance-making in students' perceptions of the classroom', *Social Psychology of* Education, 24:1, pp. 37–58.

26 Oliveira, A.W. (2010) 'Developing elementary teachers' understandings of hedges and personal pronouns in inquiry-based science classroom discourse', *Journal of Science Teacher Education*, 21:1, pp. 103–126 cited by Wilkinson, H., Putwain, D.W. & Mallaburn, A. (2020) 'How do teachers communicate to students about forthcoming GCSE exams?: An observational study', *The Psychology of Education Review*, 44:2.

27 Walker, J. M. T. (2009) 'Authoritative Classroom Management: How Control and Nurturance Work Together', *Theory Into Practice*, 48:2, pp. 122–129.

28 Collins, B., O'Connor, E., Supplee, L., & Shaw, D.S. (2017) 'Behaviour problems in elementary school among low-income boys: The role of teacher-child relationships', *Journal of Educational Research*, 110:1, pp. 72–84 and O'Connor, E., Collins, B., & Supplee, L. (2012) 'Behaviour problems in late childhood: The roles of early maternal attachment and teacher-child relationship trajectories', *Attachment & Human Development*, 14:3, pp. 265–288 cited by García-Rodríguez, L., Iriarte-Redín, C. & Reparaz-Abaitu, C. (2023) 'Teacher-student attachment relationship, variables associated, and measurement: A systematic review', *Educational Research Review,* 38.

29 Sutton, R. E., Mudrey-Camino, R., & Knight, C. C. (2009) 'Teachers' Emotion Regulation and Classroom Management', *Theory into Practice*, 48:2, pp. 130–137 and Sutton, R. E. (2004) 'Emotion regulation goals and strategies of teachers', *Social Psychology of Education*, 7, pp. 379–398.

30 Teacher Tapp (2022) 'Installing updates, behaviour, GCSEs and how many emails?!', 17 October 2002, available at: https://teachertapp.co.uk/articles/installing-updates-behaviour-gcses-how-many-emails/

31 Reid, K., Challoner, C., Lancet, A., Jones, G., Rhysiart, G. A. & Challoner, S. (2010) 'The views of Primary School Pupils at Key Stage 2 on School Behaviour in Wales', *Educational Review* 62:1, pp. 97–113.

32 Kaufmann, R. (2020) 'Negative instructor communication behaviours: exploring associations between instructor misbehaviours and the classroom learning environment', *Learning Environments Research*, 23:2, pp. 185–193.

33 McPherson, M.B., Kearney, P., & Plax, T.G. (2003) 'The dark side of instruction: teacher anger as classroom norm violations', *Journal of Applied Communication Research*, 31:1, pp. 76–90.

34 Wanzer, M.B., Frymier, A.B., Wojtaszczyk, A.M., & Smith, T. (2006) 'Appropriate and inappropriate uses of humour by teachers', *Communication Education*, 55, pp. 178–196.

35 Banas, J. A., Dunbar, N., Rodriguez, D., & Liu, S-J. (2011) 'A Review of Humour in Educational Settings: Four Decades of Research', *Communication Education*, 60:1, pp. 115–144.

36 Infantino, J. & Little, E. (2005), 'Students' Perceptions of Classroom Behaviour Problems and the Effectiveness of Different Disciplinary Methods', *Educational Psychology*, 25:5, pp. 491–508.

37 See, for example, Houghton, S., Merrett, F., & Wheldall, K. (1988) 'The attitudes of British secondary school pupils to praise, rewards, punishments and reprimands: A

further study', *New Zealand Journal of Educational Studies*, 23:2, pp. 203–214; Leach, D.J., & Tan, R. (1996) 'The Effects of Sending Positive and Negative Letters to Parents on the Classroom Behaviour of Secondary School Students', *Educational Psychology*, 16, pp. 141–154; Merrett, F., & Tang, W.M. (1994) 'The attitudes of British primary school pupils to praise, rewards, punishments and reprimands', *British Journal of Educational Psychology*, 64, pp. 91–103.

38 Infantino, J. & Little, E. (2005), 'Students' Perceptions of Classroom Behaviour Problems and the Effectiveness of Different Disciplinary Methods', *Educational Psychology*, 25:5, pp. 491–508.

39 Lewis, R. (2001) 'Classroom discipline and student responsibility: The students' view', *Teaching and Teacher Education*, 17, pp. 307–319 cited by Sutton, R. E., Mudrey-Camino, R., & Knight, C. C. (2009) 'Teachers' Emotion Regulation and Classroom Management', *Theory into Practice*, 48:2, pp. 130–137.

40 Dilekmen, M. (2011) 'Student teachers' observations of unfavourable teacher behaviours exhibited in classrooms', *Psychological Reports*, 108:1, pp. 45–53 cited by Dulay, S., & Karadağ, E. (2020) 'Undesired behaviours of secondary school teachers and their effects on students', *İlköğretim Online*, 19, pp. 2249–2269.

41 Murphy, A., & Van Brunt, B. (2018) 'Addressing dangerous behaviour in the classroom: A three-pronged approach can help educators prevent or de-escalate classroom crises', *Educational Leadership*, 76:1, pp. 66–70.

42 Clunies-Ross, P., Little, E., & Kienhuis, M. (2008) 'Self-reported and actual use of proactive and reactive classroom management strategies and their relationship with teacher stress and student behaviour', *Educational Psychology*, 28, pp. 693–710; Colvin, G., Kameenui, E. J., & Sugai, G. (1993) 'Reconceptualizing behaviour management and school-wide discipline in general education', *Education and Treatment of Children*, 16:4, pp. 361–381 cited by Thompson, A. M., & Webber, K. C. (2010) 'Realigning student and teacher perceptions of school rules: A behaviour management strategy for students with challenging behaviours', *Children & Schools*, 32:2, pp. 71–79.

43 Clunies-Ross, P., Little, E., & Kienhuis, M. (2008) 'Self-reported and actual use of proactive and reactive classroom management strategies and their relationship with teacher stress and student behaviour', *Educational Psychology*, 28, pp. 693–710.

44 Hall, J. A., Rosenthal, R., Archer, D., DiMatteo, M. R. & Rogers, P. L. (1977) 'Nonverbal skills in the classroom', *Theory into Practice*, 16:3, pp. 162–166.

45 Zeki, C.P. (2009) 'The importance of non-verbal communication in classroom management', *Procedia - Social and Behavioural Sciences*, 1, pp. 1443–1449 citing Santrock, J. (2001) *Educational psychology*, New York: McGraw Hill.

46 Ibid., citing Ledbury, R., White, I., & Dran, S. (2004) 'The Importance of Eye Contact in the Classroom', *The Internet TESL Journal*, 10:8.

47 Lyberg-Åhlander, V., Rydell, R., Löfqvist, A., Pelegrin-Garcia, D., & Brunskog, J. (2015) 'Teachers' voice use in teaching environment: aspects on speakers' comfort', *Energy Procedia*, 78, pp. 3090-3095.

48 Dhaem, J. (2012) 'Responding to Minor Misbehaviour through Verbal and Nonverbal Responses', *Beyond Behaviour*, 21:3, pp. 29–34.

49 Kraft M. A., & Monti-Nussbaum M. (2021) 'The Big Problem with Little Interruptions to Classroom Learning', *AERA Open*, 7:1, pp. 1–21.

50 Dhaem, J. (2012) 'Responding to Minor Misbehaviour through Verbal and Nonverbal Responses', *Beyond Behaviour*, 21:3, pp. 29–34.

51 Ibid

52 Infantino, J. & Little, E. (2005), 'Students' Perceptions of Classroom Behaviour Problems and the Effectiveness of Different Disciplinary Methods', *Educational Psychology*, 25:5, pp. 491–508.

53 Houghton, S., Wheldhall, K., Jukes, R., & Sharpe, A. (1990) 'The effects of limited private reprimands and increased private praise on classroom behaviour in four British secondary school classes', *British Journal of Educational Psychology*, 60, pp. 255–265.
54 Burnett, P. C. (2002) 'Teacher praise and feedback and students' perceptions of the classroom environment', *Educational Psychology*, 22:1, pp. 1–16.
55 Stipek,D.(2010)'Howdoteachers'expectationsaffectstudentlearning?',Availableat:http://www.education.com/reference/article/teachers-expectations-affect-learning/ (Accessed 11th April 2020).
56 Skipper, Y., & Douglas, K. (2015) 'The influence of teacher feedback on children's perceptions of student–teacher relationships', *British Journal of Educational Psychology*, 85, pp. 276–288.
57 Dhaem, J. (2012) 'Responding to Minor Misbehaviour through Verbal and Nonverbal Responses', *Beyond Behaviour*, 21:3, pp. 29–34.
58 See, for example, Sarver, D.E., Rapport, M.D., Kofler, M.J., Raiker, J.S. & Friedman, L.M. (2015) 'Hyperactivity in Attention-Deficit/Hyperactivity Disorder (ADHD): Impairing Deficit or Compensatory Behaviour?', *Journal of Abnormal Child Psychology*, 43, pp. 1219–1232.
59 Andrade, J. (2009) 'What does doodling do?', *Applied Cognitive Psychology*, 24:1, pp. 100-106.
60 Tadayon, M., & Afhami, R. (2016) 'Doodling Effects on Junior High School Students' Learning', *International Journal of Art & Design Education*, 36:1, pp. 118–125.
61 Arney, K. (Host). (2019, December 31) 'Fidget on Four' [Audio podcast], BBC Radio Four, available at https:// https://www.bbc.co.uk/sounds/play/m000cmyz
62 Ibid.
63 Ibid.
64 Ibid.
65 Ibid.
66 Ibid.
67 Ibid.

PART A
What can I say?

The student who keeps turning up late (#1)

The scenario

The class is seated, settled and quietly getting on with the lesson starter. Well, not quite the full class, of course. One seat remains noticeably and predictably unoccupied. As the seconds hand ticks on, you make a mental note of their increasing tardiness. One minute late. Three minutes late. Finally, after 5 minutes, the student saunters through the door.

Oscar Wilde once said that "punctuality is the thief of time." But witty aphorisms are of little use to a teacher who faces regular lesson disruption by a student turning up late. As far as you're concerned, the only robbery taking place here is students being deprived of the vital learning opportunity that takes place at the beginning of a lesson.

So how should you deal with poor punctuality?

 DOI: 10.4324/9781003440826-3

Avoid saying

"Why are you late this time?"

Reframe for success

"I'll speak to you shortly about where you've been."

Why does this work?

In these circumstances, the priority is getting the late student into their seat and on task as quickly and as quietly as possible. A public interrogation of the student, commencing the second they step through the door, is a tempting exercise. Questioning a student in this way, however, can take longer than expected. Excuses can become interminable. Tempers can become frayed. Students can become distracted by the cross-examination and the endless wait for the next stage of the lesson.

By contrast, a low-key acknowledgement of their arrival keeps the lesson on track and allows you to follow up later, away from the glare of the classroom audience. This means that if sanctions do need to be given at the end of the lesson, the student is deprived of the oxygen of social kudos that frequent latecomers often seek.

Next steps

1. **Avoid sarcastic comments –** Phrases like "I'm glad you were able to finally join us" might offer an outlet for your frustration but are very unlikely to encourage a student to turn up on time. If you're really annoyed, ignore them completely until later.

2. **Check with colleagues –** Students often lay the blame for their sluggishness on teaching colleagues. When you say you'll verify their excuse, make sure you do follow it up. They'll be less likely to use this excuse again.

3. **Anticipate recurring excuses –** Other common excuses, such as lack of equipment, can be headed off by making it known that you always have a spare pencil or calculator in your room. Contact parents or pastoral staff to ensure students have these items in future.

The student who keeps shouting out (#2)

The scenario

Whenever you're speaking to the class – be it during questioning, explanations or giving out basic instructions – you find yourself speeding up slightly. You're not anxious and rushing because of nerves. You're not trying to squeeze a few ideas in before the toll of the bell. You're not one of those people who just speaks too quickly.

What worries you is getting your words out before the inevitable interruption – the inevitable interruption from the student who repeatedly breaks the golden rule of any well-run classroom: no shouting out. It might be a desire to show off their knowledge. It might be an eagerness to join in. It might be a sense of entitlement that their voice carries more weight than their peers. It might be just to annoy you.

Whatever the cause, how can you make it stop?

DOI: 10.4324/9781003440826-4

Avoid saying

"[Student's name], stop shouting out."

Reframe for success

"Let me remind everyone of my expectations: if you want to speak, you must raise your hand first."

Why does this work?

Personalised comments about poor behaviour have several unwanted consequences. First, drawing attention to the student can backfire if they want to publicly display their disruptive behaviour. Second, highlighting a single student can provoke confrontation. Third, when the student's name is said in an exasperated tone, it pours further fuel on the fire.

By contrast, a calm but direct focus on desired conduct, rather than pinpointing students who aren't following the classroom rules, is far more likely to lead to a reduction in shouting out. Shouting out must *always* be tackled. Yet repeated reminders of this nature help to build a much more positive classroom atmosphere than naming individuals.

Next steps

1. **Ignore then acknowledge answers –** Ignore correct but shouted out answers. Once another correct answer is given elsewhere, acknowledge the initial correct response but explain that, unfortunately, it didn't follow the hands-up format.
2. **Use non-verbal signals –** The universal gesture for "be quiet" (#81) works equally well for students who shout out. Using this non-verbal reminder avoids breaking the flow of your explanations and questioning.
3. **Give low-key warnings –** For consistent offenders, follow the behaviour policy and give warnings as appropriate. Where possible, do this without any kind of fanfare, e.g. silently write their name on the board or whisper the warning in their ear as soon as you can.

The student with their head on the desk (#3)

The scenario

Like a dutiful waiter flitting from table to table, you circulate around the room, checking on the progress of your students. Some are working their way serenely through the activities. Others need a bit of assistance, in the form of a scaffolded explanation or question of clarification. The atmosphere is studious; there's a sense of purpose in the room.

But then you come to a student whose somnolent body language suggests a total lack of commitment to the tasks you've set. Slouched over the desk, their forehead rests upon the worksheet you've spent your precious PPA (planning, preparation and assessment) time creating. As you approach, they open their eyes and prise their head from the table with some reluctance.

What should you say to a student like this?

DOI: 10.4324/9781003440826-5

Avoid saying

"Get on with your work now!"

Reframe for success

"Right, let's have a look at where you've got up to."

Why does this work?

A common frustration for students is when teachers presume they're being lazy when they are, in reality, just stuck. It's understandable that a student's languorous posture would lead a teacher to perceive their inactivity as work-avoidance. But, unless you're sure that they're dodging work, jumping to conclusions demotivates struggling students further.

By assuming good intent on the student's part, you're demonstrating you're there to help rather than immediately believing the worst of them. Through a focus on what is stopping them from completing the work, you put the emphasis on getting back on track instead of dealing with an apparent behaviour concern. In the long run, this tends to encourage them to persevere with work rather than dropping their head to the desk in resignation.

Next steps

1. **Are they stuck or sleepy?** – An alternative explanation for their inertia may be straightforward tiredness. If this is the real problem, inform parents and address the issue of sleepiness (#59).
2. **Check in on these students first** – Allow a few minutes for the class to attempt the work, then prioritise students who tend to lose focus when stuck. This will enable you to confirm whether they really are struggling or are merely avoiding work, in which case sanctions will need to follow.
3. **Agree subtle signals for when they need help** – Students can be reluctant to ask for help due to fears about appearing stupid. Rather than expecting them to call across the room, give them a discreet signal to use to ask for help when necessary.

The class that uses unkind "banter" (#4)

The scenario

Given the opportunity, some members of your class use words like weapons. These weapons don't take the form of a full-scale bombardment. We aren't talking rocket-propelled grenades and short-range missiles here; no red buttons are pushed, no payloads released. These students employ a more subtle form of warfare.

Rejecting outright attacks, they prefer to adopt the guise of comedy for their guerrilla tactics. Jokey barbs and snide gags are the currency of conflict. Friends make friends laugh at the expense of other friends. Friends insult friends until they sometimes stop being friends. When challenged, they insist that "it's just banter." They weren't being serious.

How should you deal with this insidious "humour"?

DOI: 10.4324/9781003440826-6

Avoid saying

"That's enough – banter is banned in this class."

Reframe for success

"It doesn't matter whether you were trying to be hurtful or not. When our words cause upset, there are consequences."

Why does this work?

If we're not careful, "Banter" can be used as a euphemism to excuse the wide-ranging methods employed by young people to embarrass their peers. This might take the form of mockery, unpleasant "pranks" and verbal insults. Trying to combat this, teachers might quite reasonably want to ban banter – zero tolerance to jokey behaviour of any sort.

Unfortunately, bans of this kind are ineffective. Instead of attempting to censor students' humour, a more productive use of our time is helping them to understand the impact of their words. Discussing the harmful consequences of their throwaway comments can encourage them to follow a gentler path, where humour lifts rather than drags us down.

Next steps

1. **Limit discussions if necessary –** Classes tend to enjoy debates about interesting issues that are thrown up by a topic. Make it clear, however, that these discussions will only take place if students make mature and considerate contributions.

2. **Reject gender stereotypes –** Boys do tend to be more attracted to unkind banter than girls. But using the "boys will be boys" excuse is unacceptable. Teaching young males about the effects of mean jokes is an important aspect of our role.

3. **Don't become an accomplice –** Ever used a funny but withering comment to put a cheeky student firmly in their place? Your sarcastic retort might get a laugh from the rest of the class, but it will likely damage your relationships with the student. What's more, it will also encourage the rest of the class to view humiliation through humour as a valid brand of communication in your classroom.

The student who is a persistent pen tapper (#5)

The scenario

All eyes are focused on you. The class is silent. Your voice carries clearly through the air; there's no noise to compete with. You have the students' complete attention. Then, almost imperceptibly, a faint noise emerges. Initially, it is almost inaudible, like the tip of a fingernail being very gently but repeatedly struck against a window pane. Soon, however, it becomes increasingly noticeable.

A student sits at a nearby desk. Having deconstructed then reassembled their pen, they're now tapping out some indecipherable Morse code on the table. By now, the noise is more than an irritant: the class is becoming less focussed and, against the backdrop of the nib's repetitive beats, you've forgotten what you were saying.

DOI: 10.4324/9781003440826-7

Avoid saying

"Can you please stop doing that!"

Reframe for success

"A reminder that all pens need to be down while I'm speaking."

Why does this work?

For some students, pen tapping is a deliberately disruptive strategy, designed to display to their peers that they are reluctant to pay attention. In this case, the noise is designed to be irksome, gradually becoming louder as a test of your patience. For other students, however, pen tapping is unintentional, a natural "fidgety" movement that they aren't always aware that they're doing.

Either way, publicly reprimanding the student is unlikely to improve the situation. The deliberate disruptor will gain social recognition, while the unintentional disruptor will feel unfairly treated. A much more effective approach is to depersonalise your reminder of expectations to the class in a clear and calm manner.

Next steps

1. **Frontload instructions about pens –** To establish routines that discourage pen tapping, remind students "pens down, look at me" before giving other instructions. Over time, this should become automatic.
2. **Circulate and place the pen on the desk –** Avoid interrupting the flow of your lesson by continuing to talk while walking towards the student, then politely motioning for them to give you the pen. Next, place it on the desk but away from their hands.
3. **Suggest inaudible alternatives –** Sit down with "fidgety" tappers and discuss alternatives that don't get in the way of other students' focus. A finger tapped on the palm, for example, is much quieter.

The class that misbehaves for cover teachers (#6)

The scenario

It's taken a while, but you've managed to get this class right where you want them. After lots of routine building, and plenty of restating expectations, you've moulded them into a sharply focused, consistently well-behaved unit. It hasn't been easy, but it's been worth it.

Until one day you return from an absence and find a terse note on your desk. The teacher who has covered for you was not at all impressed with their behaviour. The note – well, it's more of a dossier, to be honest – outlines the unacceptable work ethic and conduct of a sizeable number of students.

How should you approach this particular situation?

DOI: 10.4324/9781003440826-8

Avoid saying	Reframe for success
"Let's not worry too much about yesterday's lesson."	"Your behaviour in my absence is just as important as when I'm teaching you."

Why does this work?

When your class misbehaves for another teacher, it can be tempting to turn a blind eye. After all, they behave well for you. So is it such a big deal if they lower their standards for an adult they haven't had the chance to build a relationship with? You've spent a lot of effort shaping them into a studious unit. Why risk ruining that rapport over a teacher they might not have again?

This attitude is misguided and somewhat selfish for several reasons. First, if they were messing around, they weren't doing the work you set them, which is indirectly disrespecting you. Second, by not treating poor behaviour in your absence as a serious matter, you are giving them the green light to behave like this for other unsuspecting teachers. And third, this class represents you when you're not there; they need to see good behaviour for cover teachers as an extension of your expectations.

Next steps

1. **Liaise with the cover teacher –** Where necessary, clarify what took place and which students need to be dealt with. Ask them for their opinion about what they would like to happen next.

2. **Apply sanctions as normal –** Work that was not completed should be finished as extra homework. Unacceptable behaviour should be addressed as it would be in normal circumstances.

3. **Remind students of what you expect before a planned absence –** In situations where you know you'll be away from school, let them know in advance and reinforce your expectations rigorously.

The class that always ask to go to the toilet (#7)

The scenario

It's not long after break, and the next lesson is underway. You're in the middle of explaining a complex idea when a student pops their hand up. Expecting them to ask for clarification or raise an interesting point, you pause and allow them to speak. Their important question? "Can I go to the toilet, please?"

Now, let's be clear, this is frustrating for several reasons. First, they should have gone during the recent break. Second, they've interrupted your vital explanation with something unrelated to the work. Finally, this question will set a precedent: give them permission to go and you'll be inviting a potential string of toilet requests from other students.

What's the best course of action?

DOI: 10.4324/9781003440826-9

Avoid saying	**Reframe for success**
"You're just going to have to hold it in."	"I will let you go on this occasion, but this will not be something that happens regularly."

Why does this work?

Deciding whether to let students go to the toilet during lessons is arguably the most difficult judgement call a teacher is often asked to make. Allow students to take frequent visits to the bathroom and you'll be setting yourself up for a revolving door of mini-truancy during your lessons. Deny students this basic biological function and you could well end up dealing with the consequences of a student being sick on your floor, or worse.

On balance, the least-worst option is to let students use the toilet but to express your dissatisfaction that they need to go during lessons. This situation is far from ideal, but by making it clear to the class that you do not expect repeated requests for the bathroom, you can strongly discourage these breaks becoming the norm in your classroom.

Next steps

1. **Explain the consequences of missed lesson time** – Five minutes absence from the lesson can be crucial, leading to misunderstanding and misconceptions. Talk to your class about why going at break time helps them learn better in the long term.
2. **Notice student trends** – Is this a flustered student who's never before asked for a bathroom break? Or a student who routinely asks to go during every lesson? Spot patterns and liaise with pastoral leads to address any recurring issues.
3. **Don't allow them to go in groups** – If two students need the toilet, avoid letting them go at the same time. This can help reduce instances of poor behaviour and possible safeguarding issues happening in the toilets.

The student who argues back (#8)

The scenario

They are waiting. They are ready. They are looking for an opportunity. Whenever you challenge them about their behaviour – be it turning around, talking over you, not focusing on their work – it always leads to further problems. It's got to the stage where, fearful of a volcanic escalation, you sometimes choose to ignore behaviours that you'd normally tackle.

Each time follows a similar, dismal pattern. You spot this student doing something they shouldn't be doing, and you call them out on it. Whether it's a mild rebuke or a full-blown warning, the result is the same: they argue back vociferously. They weren't doing anything wrong. So and so was doing it too. Why are you always picking on them?

How can you break this cycle of conflict?

DOI: 10.4324/9781003440826-10

Avoid saying

"[Student's name], stop talking!"

Reframe for success

"I'm just waiting for some of you to remember my expectations. While I'm speaking, nobody else talks."

Why does this work?

Mentioning specific students by name runs the risk of provoking a teacher/student stand-off. Over time, the classroom can be the scene of everyday skirmishes. Drawing attention to the student may also unintentionally reward them with social kudos gained by battling it out with the teacher.

Depersonalising and pluralising the situation, by contrast, removes the gladiatorial element. Rather than the reprimand of a named individual, there's a calm but direct reminder of universal expectations. The source of disruption may be obvious, but this subtle shift to generalised expectation means a showdown is far less likely.

Next steps

1. **Avoid public confrontation** – Removing the audience is paramount in this context. Wherever possible, offer discreet challenges and whispered warnings to the student. Ask them to briefly step outside where longer lectures are necessary.

2. **Offer a social time discussion** – When students continue to protest after being censured, explain that you are happy to discuss it in detail during social time. More often than not, the implicit loss of their break time is enough to quieten the student.

3. **Use non-verbals** – Dropping the student's name is very effective. But perhaps even more so is the use of gestures (e.g. "stop talking" #81). By removing the vocal element, you are able to use less intrusive signals, which again deprives the student of the chance to argue back.

The class that likes to wrestle and bump into each other (#9)

The scenario

We now go live to Madison Square Gardens, New York. It's time to hand over to your MC for the evening, Mikey "The Mouth" Bell:

> Laaaadies and gentullllmennn. In the Blue Corner, our challenger is a young fighter weighing in at 97 pounds (taking into account a bag full of exercise books, packed lunch and 13 leaking pens). Annnnd in the Red Corner, the reigning, undisputed Champion of the Worrrrrrrrld, weighing in at 103 pounds (if we include his PE kit and puffer coat). Letttttt's get readddddy to rumble!

Wrestling might be innocent entertainment on television. But in your classroom, it's a real nuisance. How can you stop students acting rough for fun?

DOI: 10.4324/9781003440826-11

Avoid saying	Reframe for success
"If you want to hug each other, do it in your own time!"	"Everyone standing behind desks until I dismiss you."

Why does this work?

Unless your classroom is a scene of total disorder, playful jostling tends to occur at certain stages of a lesson. First, as students enter the classroom. Second, if they need to move around the classroom during practical activities. Third, at the end of the lesson as they await the bell. Remaining vigilant during these lesson transitions is key.

It can be tempting to use sarcastic humour in these circumstances. But any joke that implies a romantic attraction between friends – especially if they are of the same sex – can backfire spectacularly. Instead, minimise opportunities for students to be in close proximity to one another by carefully monitoring likely combatants as the class enter, leave or move around.

Next steps

1. **Meet, greet and observe** – As you welcome the class in, position your body so that you can twist between viewing the incoming line of students and keeping an eye on those already in the room. Direct students to sit down immediately as they enter.

2. **Dismiss a row or table at a time** – Crowded doorways are perfect wrestling hotspots. Avoid congestion and keep things orderly by dismissing students in small groups.

3. **Evaluate offers from volunteers** – Using students to hand out and collect in lesson materials can be a very helpful timesaver. Some students, however, will offer to do this for the opportunity to partake in a playful scuffle. Turn down offers from students who go rogue when collecting in the glue sticks.

The class that packs up before you're finished (#10)

The scenario

As the large clock hand edges its way perceptibly towards the end of lesson time, the class becomes restless. Attention starts to drift away from you and towards the ticking clock. Exercise books are closed. Booklets slipped into folders. Lids placed decisively back on pen nibs.

Spurred on by cues from the earliest downers of tools, the rest of the class begin to follow their lead. Before too long, the gradual drip of items being discreetly put away has become a veritable tsunami of packing up. Like hungry mouths, unzipped bags start consuming the leftover books and worksheets.

How can you prevent this rude interruption to the important last few minutes of your lesson?

DOI: 10.4324/9781003440826-12

Avoid saying

"Did I tell you to pack up? No, well get your stuff back out!"

Reframe for success

"In a moment, it will be time to pack up. But for now, you need to listen to this final point."

Why does this work?

Students become attuned to the timings and rhythms of the school day. Inevitably, they sense when a lesson is nearing its close and start to think about what comes next. Minds drift towards things like food or the subject of the following lesson. To address this issue, therefore, teachers need to be alert to the initial stages of this scenario, noticing subtle shifts in student focus before they crescendo to the disorder described above.

Signalling that the end is nigh, but that you need their attention for a crucial, final few moments, is important. By front loading this instruction, you're acknowledging their restlessness but prioritising your vital last point.

Next steps

1. **Give them time to pack up –** If you don't allow a reasonable amount of time for students to pack up before the bell sounds, they'll naturally try and steal a minute here and there. Keep an eye on the clock and finish punctually where possible.

2. **Save your breath after the bell –** In my experience, once the bell goes you've generally lost their attention from thereafter. Trying to give clear instructions about things like homework, in this context, is likely to end badly.

3. **Review rushed lesson endings –** Where lessons do end in a rush of chaos, make sure you go back next lesson and review what you were covering as the bell went. Otherwise, important points will probably be ignored.

The student who is late to ask for homework help (#11)

The scenario

It's the start of the school day. Walking down the corridor towards your classroom, you encounter a slightly red-faced student. Hesitantly, they explain the problem. They need some help for that piece of homework that you set last week. That piece of homework you set last week, which is due today. They're stuck. They're not sure where to begin. They haven't done it.

This leaves you in a tricky situation. Option A: rebuke the student and send them away, with the follow-up consequence of a detention for non-completion of homework. Option B: give them the help they require to finish the homework and extend the deadline by one day to allow them to finish the task.

Which option should you choose?

DOI: 10.4324/9781003440826-13

Avoid saying

"Why didn't you come and see me last week? It's too late asking for help now."

Reframe for success

"It would've been much better if you'd have come and seen me last week but let me explain what you need to do."

Why does this work?

There is one common reason why students are reluctant to seek help: embarrassment. Students tend not to ask for help because they worry that their teachers, and their peers, will think they are stupid. It can take a lot, therefore, to summon up the courage to admit that they don't know how to do the work, and to seek assistance from their teacher. And if the teacher castigates them and dismisses them, they are unlikely to put themselves through the ordeal again any time soon.

Despite our frustrations, we need to prioritise responding to a request for help over a fixed homework deadline. By doing this we are sending out the signal that asking for help, and admitting when we are stuck, is a fruitful long-term strategy.

Next steps

1. **Normalise help-seeking –** To encourage students to come to you for help, talk about the strategies you would use if stuck on the homework you are setting. This helps students to see that struggle and help-seeking are central to the learning process.

2. **Stop asking "Any questions?" –** Because students generally don't like asking for help, they are unlikely to respond to your "Any questions?" request. Instead, give them a post-it note to write down things they don't understand anonymously.

3. **Tackle persistent homework lateness –** If students continue to miss deadlines, follow the usual sanction process. There's only so many times they can use "I need your help" as a Get Out of Detention Free card.

The student who comes into class in the wrong uniform (#12)

The scenario

It's every single lesson. They turn up at the door wearing an item of non-uniform clothing. The garment in question might well be fashionable and comfortable but it's expressly forbidden by school policy. It might be a basketball hoody. It might be a puffer jacket. It might be a rather nice cashmere scarf. Whatever it is, it's got to come off.

But as soon as you challenge the student, things escalate. Your instruction to remove it leads to an outburst of frustration. An outburst of frustration leads to a formal warning. A formal warning leads to them shouting at you and being removed from the lesson. All because they just wouldn't take off a sweatshirt.

How could this situation be avoided?

DOI: 10.4324/9781003440826-14

Avoid saying	Reframe for success
"That's coming off before you come into my lesson."	"Come on in, take a seat. As we get started, let's also make sure our uniform is sorted out."

Why does this work?

From the student's perception, all you care about is immediately picking up on a uniform infringement. The initial interaction – a request to take it off – starts each lesson with a negative. For some students, this is all it takes to trigger a chain of events like the scenario described above.

By greeting them with a polite smile and getting them in the room, you start with a positive foundation from which to tackle the uniform violation. Let's be clear: the offending item is coming off! You're not going to ignore the uniform policy. By getting them settled and working, however, and then discreetly asking them to remove it after a couple of minutes, invariably, you'll find they comply without much fuss.

Next steps

1. **Use a non-verbal instruction –** Rather than telling them to take the item off, give them a subtle signal by tugging at your own jumper, or taking off your own (imaginary) coat. This non-confrontational approach usually does the trick.

2. **Give thinking/cooling off time –** If students stubbornly refuse to fix their uniform after a quiet request, calmly spell out the potential consequences and give them time to make the sensible decision.

3. **Ask for pastoral support –** Ideally, a teacher shouldn't have to deal with this scenario in the first place. Speak to the student's tutor, head of year or SLT link. Can this uniform issue be addressed at the start of the day, so classroom teachers don't have to tackle it?

The class that ridicules other students' contributions (#13)

The scenario

As a teacher, one of the things you feel passionately about is sharing students' ideas with the rest of the class. Through careful questioning, you are able to elicit thoughtful responses for other students to build on. By using students' work, you are able to showcase excellence and highlight areas for improvement.

But with this particular class, your efforts to include more student contributions are backfiring. When you place a student's book under the visualiser, or ask them to explain their thoughts in detail, you encounter regular laughter of the mocking variety. Consequently, students show an understandable reticence towards sharing their work or answering complex questions.

How can you reset this unpleasant classroom culture?

DOI: 10.4324/9781003440826-15

Avoid saying

"I don't know why you're laughing. I doubt you could do any better."

Reframe for success

"We learn so much more as a class when we share our work and respond respectfully. I don't expect to hear anything other than helpful comments."

Why does this work?

With immature classes, building a supportive classroom environment takes time and lots of reminders about how to show respect towards their peers. Some students move quickly from gentle ribbing to unpleasant mockery. Tempting though it may be, embarrassing these students about their contributions will only heighten the antagonistic nature of the class.

Instead, give frequent reminders about what helpful feedback looks like. Model kindness and courtesy when critiquing student responses. Highlight the benefits of sharing ideas. Encourage students to offer an honest appraisal of your contributions and thank them for their considerate opinions. Over time, the class will start to take each other more seriously.

Next steps

1. **Praise work rather than individuals** – Focus on ideas ("what I really like about that idea is …") rather than making it about the person who has produced it. By shifting the emphasis away from individuals, more students will feel comfortable joining in.

2. **Don't just rely on volunteers** – In classes where only the keenest, most confident students share their work, nuggets of brilliance by quieter students are likely to remain unmined. "Borrow" their work and share it anonymously to begin with.

3. **Always check first** – Be careful about sharing a student's work without reading it carefully. It may have illegible handwriting, which you'll awkwardly stumble over, or it might include something in the answer that you'd rather not publicise.

The student who responds "don't know" to questions (#14)

The scenario

To ensure all students are thinking hard and participating fully in your lesson, you use cold call as your default questioning strategy. As a result, responses to your questions aren't dominated by very keen or very smart students. Students expect to be called upon during questioning. The majority are happy to comply with this.

But one student isn't having any of it. Routinely, they respond to your questions with a pained expression or an indifferent shrug. No matter how nicely you ask the question, the standard response is a grunted "dunno".

What can you do to get them answering?

DOI: 10.4324/9781003440826-16

Avoid saying

"Ok. Does anybody else know the answer?"

Reframe for success

"You might not *know* the answer but what do you *think*?"

Why does this work?

There are numerous reasons why a student might say "don't know" to a question. It may be that your question was badly worded. It might have required prior knowledge that the student doesn't yet possess. It might be that you didn't give them long enough wait time and pressed them too quickly for a response. It might be that they are socially awkward and are trying to discourage you from asking further questions that thrust them into the spotlight. It might just also be that it was a really hard question!

Regardless of the reason, if you accept a "dunno" without further probing, you'll advertise to the rest of the class that it's fine to repeatedly duck out of answering questions. Instead, you need to ensure that students at least attempt an answer before you move on.

Next steps

1. **Scaffold questions –** To help make questions easier to understand, go back and rephrase in a way that offers a helpful prompt or narrows the focus down by offering options.

2. **Use think/pair/share before questioning –** Giving students the opportunity to discuss a tricky question in advance allows them to formulate their ideas more clearly before responding in front of the class individually.

3. **Get them to repeat the correct answer –** If you get the sense that the student is using "don't know" as an opportunity to opt out of participating fully in the lesson, you need to show that not giving an answer is not acceptable. Once a correct answer is given, go back to the reluctant responder and make them repeat the right answer. This will encourage them to offer a contribution in future.

The student who constantly fidgets (#15)

The scenario

How does this student fidget? Here are the ways. First, they're rarely still. Wriggling in their seat like an eel in a bucket, they seem incapable of remaining stationary for two minutes. Next there's the fiddling with pens. Not just tapping. No, they dismantle them until springs fly across the room or their hands look like a blue ink version of Lady Macbeth's.

If it's not Biro fiddling, it's tearing slender strips of paper from the bottom of worksheets, ready to be shaped into a tiny sphere. Then, inevitably, there's the fidget toy – a lurid purple spinner or a rainbow-coloured cube – which causes repeated disruption when passed around among nearby students like contraband. Then there's glue sticks, erasers…

Is there something you can do to stop this fidgetiness?

DOI: 10.4324/9781003440826-17

Avoid saying	Reframe for success
"[Student's name], sit still and stop fidgeting!"	"Everyone looking this way. Nobody should be holding glue sticks or paper at this stage."

Why does this work?

For some students – such as those diagnosed with ADHD (attention deficit hyperactivity disorder) – body and hand movement can be difficult to control. Indeed, fidgeting is often used by these students as a method to *maintain* concentration. Simply telling them to keep their body and hands stationary is unlikely to improve their attention. The mental load required to concentrate on sitting still will leave less attention for focusing on the work in front of them.

A balance needs to be struck between recognising some students' need to fidget and ensuring that they, and importantly their classmates, aren't distracted by this movement. A reasonable adjustment is to allow restless students to fidget discreetly but to step in when this hinders their concentration or distracts their peers. Fiddling in silence with a small tool under the desk while listening to you is fine, turning around and sharing toys with other students is unacceptable. Swaying gently in their chair while completing work is ok, ripping up the worksheet and flicking paper about the room is definitely not.

Next steps

1. **Share your observations privately –** Students may need help recognising what distracts them and what doesn't. Point out occasions when you noticed that playing with certain things stopped them working, while other things helped them focus.
2. **Use subtle recognition –** Give a quick thumbs up signal (#88), or have a quiet word, to tell them you're impressed when they've made efforts to improve their attention.
3. **Employ very brief rest breaks –** Where hyperactivity continues to be an issue, allow the student the opportunity to step out of the classroom for a minute or so. Monitor this carefully to ensure it isn't abused and aids rather than disrupts.

The class that shouts across the room to each other (#16)

The scenario

Like a chess grandmaster studying obscure game openings, you were meticulous in your planning. Colour coded and rigorously researched, your seating plan was destined to make a difference. The result of many hours of mental labours, it was designed to nullify bad influences, separate unproductive partnerships and stop some students killing each other.

What looked perfect on paper, however, has failed in practice. By banishing the "characters" to the four corners of the classroom, you haven't diluted the sway they have over their peers. Instead of chatting to each other, all that happens is when they're meant to be working quietly they just shout to one another across the room. It's a nightmare.

How can you prevent these vocal students from wrecking your lessons?

DOI: 10.4324/9781003440826-18

Avoid saying	Reframe for success
"I can hardly hear myself think. Stop shouting!"	"The only noise I expect to hear is students occasionally whispering to their partners about the work. If I'm not happy with the volume levels, I will insist on total silence."

Why does this work?

Despite our hard work and good intentions, there are times when best-laid plans go awry. When a seating plan fails to address significant disruption from a strident minority, we have to revert to plan B. Requests to "stop shouting" are unlikely to prevent students from shouting. A much more specific instruction is required to remove the opportunity to disrupt.

When students behave in this coordinated manner, there is no alternative than to insist on silence or near silence. This is the only way that you will be able to keep a close eye on who is making this unacceptable noise. By standing in a convenient position and monitoring the four corners like a lighthouse scanning turbulent waters, you'll reduce the general uproar.

Next steps

1. **Insist on silence during questioning** – During question and answer, ensure that full attention is given, and chatting isn't allowed to occur. Stop immediately, remind the class, then warn each time this happens to prevent further shouting across the room.

2. **Don't allow levels to increase when watching clips** – Teachers often lower their guard when watching a video clip, reasoning that the volume levels will drown out any off-task noise. This is a mistake. Expect the same standards whether it's you or a documentary doing the explaining.

3. **Remove repeat offenders** – Ultimately, students need to recognise that your classroom is a place for focused learning and that disruptive noise can't be tolerated. Some activities will, of course, generate higher noise levels, but even then there is no place for bellowing in the classroom. If they don't comply, they must be removed.

The student who never completes all the tasks (#17)

The scenario

Working your way around the room, you see pleasing levels of activity. Students are busy, engaged and close to completing tasks. The questions you set are nearly done. The spaces for answers on the worksheet are adorned with ink. Empty boxes are being filled with the satisfying scrawl of letters or numbers.

Inevitably, though, when you get to a particular student's desk, this isn't the case. They've stalled at question two. Large expanses of white remain on the worksheet. Boxes are devoid of letters or numbers. Your nudges to get a move on have little impact.

What can you do to ensure this student completes your tasks?

DOI: 10.4324/9781003440826-19

Avoid saying

"Why haven't you filled in all the boxes?"

Reframe for success

"Let me give you some feedback on what you've done, so you'll be able to get going with the other tasks."

Why does this work?

Understandably, teachers love to see students working busily. Productivity is an essential part of academic success. But teachers can be blinded by an obsession with task completion as a marker of whether students are learning. Filling in boxes and answering questions can create an illusion of hard work. But students looking like they're working hard doesn't necessarily mean they're thinking hard.

Conversely, students who are not completing tasks might be working more slowly because they are grappling with more complex ideas. Assuming they are being lazy, rather than being stuck or thinking carefully about how to answer the question can lead to resentment and demotivation. It's vital, therefore, to give these students feedback on what they've achieved rather than automatically bemoaning what they haven't done.

Next steps

1. **Make feedback about the work, not the individual** – When giving feedback, emphasise how the student's understanding can be developed rather than using it as an opportunity to be critical of the student for not completing all the work.

2. **Check for deeper thinking** – Are you sure that students who complete tasks have really understood the key ideas from the worksheet? Use retrieval quizzes to discover whether their busyness is actually leading to long-term recall of knowledge.

3. **Use "the dot" to boost productivity** – If you're convinced that the student is definitely being unproductive to avoid work, motivate them to speed up by placing a dot in the margin and explain what you expect them to have completed when you return in five minutes.

The student who swears in your class (#18)

The scenario

It's been brewing for a while. Like the prelude to a thunderstorm, the classroom's atmosphere is dark, heavy and fractious. Interactions between these two students create electrical charges: it's only a question of how long before we witness a dramatic event.

Sure enough, it happens. Provocation is layered upon provocation. The antipathy is mutual. Yet, like magnetic poles they attract as much as they repel. They can't stand each other. But they can't stand not having the opportunity to wind each other up. Finally, inevitably, one snaps and poses a rhetorical profanity: "Why don't you just f*** off?"

The class goes silent. What do you do now?

DOI: 10.4324/9781003440826-20

Avoid saying	Reframe for success
"Get out of my room!"	"Ok, you need to pick up your work and go immediately to [removal room in behaviour policy]."

Why does this work?

In a well-ordered classroom, in a well-ordered school, swearing is a shocking act. As such, it can cause a rapid rise in a teacher's emotional temperature. This is especially the case where a teacher's patience is already frazzled by tit-for-tat warfare between two antagonistic students. But a yelled response will only increase the heat further.

The class is already stunned by the student's outburst. Everyone knows this is a serious behaviour issue. Shouting is unnecessary and serves only to suggest that you have lost a grip on an already volatile situation. Staying calm and simply stating where the student needs to go will reassert your control of the room. The rest of the class needs to get back to work.

Next steps

1. **Contextualise the incident** – When logging behaviour, make sure that your write-up is fair and dispassionate. Pastoral leads will need a balanced account, which notes any mitigating circumstances, before putting sanctions in place.
2. **Develop selective hearing** – Swearing that is clearly audible must be addressed. But what if you stumble across two students using what you think might be foul language during a conversation? In this case, "I hope you didn't say what I thought you said?" makes an effective point without the need for a Draconian interrogation.
3. **Stay calm if you're targeted** – If you're unlucky enough to have a student swear directly at you, in most cases they'll likely receive a suspension of some sort. Regardless, it's important that no matter how angry you are about the personal attack, keep this internal and follow the same measured approach as when expletives are used towards other students.

The class that mocks your mistakes (#19)

The scenario

It's been a busy, tiring day. As you reach the final session of the afternoon, your brain feels foggy; energy levels have dropped close to total depletion. Standing at the board, you're in the middle of explaining something, when a guffaw emerges from one side of the room. Before too long, a further laugh erupts from the opposite part of the class. You look their way, and there's momentary silence.

Soon after, as your explanation continues, a hand goes up. The smirk on the student's face implies mischief. Wearily, you ask what the problem is. You've made a very basic mistake. A common word spelled incorrectly. A simple addition mis-calculated. A historical date a few centuries out. Gleefully, the student points this out; the class sniggers as you squirm and reach for the board rubber.

How can you come back from this humiliation?

DOI: 10.4324/9781003440826-21

Avoid saying	Reframe for success
"If you think you can do better, come up and take over!"	"Thank you. Well done for spotting that mistake."

Why does this work?

Students are only able to derive pleasure from our slip-ups if we react in a defensive manner. Mistakes – especially when we are tired or preoccupied – are inevitable at some point. By rising to this immature mockery, we give students exactly what they're looking for. Passive-aggressive sarcasm is damaging to teacher/student relationships. And what happens if they take you up on your offer of leading this class? Further disruption is guaranteed.

By contrast, when we show humility and respond to these "helpful" contributions from students in a good-natured way, we advertise how we're confident enough to deal with dropping the odd blunder. The mistake happened. Now let's move on.

Next steps

1. **Adopt a grateful persona –** Thanking students for being so helpful takes away the fun of spotting your gaffes. Be unfailingly polite and they'll lose interest in this game.
2. **Critique your own work first –** To illustrate the confidence you have in your expertise, highlight sloppy mistakes you make along the way. Not only does this rob them of the opportunity to ridicule you, it also models a healthy focus on continual improvement.
3. **Work on subject knowledge weaknesses –** Teachers sometimes respond badly to student mockery when the topic they're teaching leaves them feeling out of their depth. Developing subject knowledge will reduce these feelings of inadequacy.

The student who gives in quickly when attempting tasks (#20)

The scenario

You join us at the start of this most prestigious race; it's fair to say that the buzz of tension among the crowd is palpable. After many hours of expert briefings, the team manager's work is done. Everything now comes down to the competitors. The pit lanes fall into expectant silence. Can these young drivers hold their nerve?

The green lights flash. The field flies from their grid positions. And they're off! But, wait. What is this? Almost immediately, a familiar competitor has stalled with yet another mysterious malfunction. Apparently damaged and defeated, after just a few metres, they stutter to the sideline. Once more in this inconsistent career, they seem unable to carry on.

Is there anything their manager can say to them to convince them to continue?

DOI: 10.4324/9781003440826-22

Avoid saying

"Stop being lazy and get on with your work."

Reframe for success

"Ok, tell me what you do understand about the work."

Why does this work?

The classroom, of course, is not really a grand prix. Students aren't really competitors. And learning isn't a race. But the sporting analogy is still useful in helping understand the mindset of students who tend to reach swiftly for the white flag rather than striving to reach the chequered flag.

In the vast majority of cases, it's not laziness that prevents students from finishing their own race. Rather, it's a debilitating mindset that gives in as soon as things become challenging. By labelling children (verbally or internally) as "lazy," we fail to take into account the intimidating nature of challenging work. Asking them what they do understand, and then providing guidance to enable them to begin tackling the next steps, is a much more fruitful approach.

Next steps

1. **Provide accessible models –** Having a worked example or successful paragraph on the board enables students to see a visual model of what good work looks like. Break it down into steps for students who are really struggling.

2. **Discuss sources of help in advance –** When giving task instructions, make explicit reference to steps students should take if they get stuck. This might include seeking help from a work partner, a helpful page in the textbook or timings of how long they should spend attempting the task before asking you for assistance.

3. **Talk about the importance of struggling –** Students are more likely to persevere in a classroom environment where struggle is normalised. Remind students that hitting a wall when tackling complex work is a normal, indeed essential, part of learning.

The class that asks if they can work off warnings (#21)

The scenario

Due to poor behaviour, you've been handing out warnings like a referee at a bad-tempered local derby. There's no doubt in your mind that these sanctions were fully justified. And the lack of protest from students has reassured you that the multiple warnings were deserved. Indeed, the students have accepted that their behaviour warranted the consequence.

Rather than complain, the students have moved on to damage limitation mode. Instead of pleas for mitigation you're now receiving requests for time off for good behaviour. Entering full bargaining mode, they ask whether they can work off their warnings if they are "really good" and work "really hard" for the rest of the lesson.

Should you give in to their call for leniency?

DOI: 10.4324/9781003440826-23

Avoid saying	Reframe for success
"Ok, just this once, I'll let you work your warnings off."	"You know my expectations, so the warnings will stay. But you do have the opportunity to impress me in the time we have left."

Why does this work?

Like a government refusing to negotiate with terrorists, teachers must also stand resolute and refuse to negotiate with lesson disruptors. Give in to them once and from that moment on every warning will be up for debate. From this position, it's a slippery slope towards each decision you make being queried or politely challenged. Students will spot any behavioural grey areas and exploit them as much as possible.

Some will argue that refusing to wipe off warnings risks worsening behaviour, that students have no incentive to improve their behaviour. Positive behaviour modifications can still be noted, however, in follow-up discussions with parents and pastoral staff. But the bottom line is when students have disrupted the lesson, they must face the consequences.

Next steps

1. **Explain the purpose of warnings –** Warnings may come with consequences, but they are still, in essence, a nudge for students to change their behaviour. As such, students need to understand that sensible warnings are there to help them.

2. **Give pre-warning reminders –** Before handing out a raft of warnings, let students know that they are imminent. Writing and underlining the word "warnings" on the board acts as a helpful visual signal that your patience is expiring.

3. **Keep a tally of persistent disruptors –** If you don't log warnings on a behaviour system, keep your own record of students who are racking up multiple warnings before pulling back. These issues need to be addressed, even if they're not being removed from the room.

The class that ostracises a student (#22)

The scenario

Some of your students are expert at riding the wave of popularity. Like sure-footed surfers, they negotiate powerful white breakers with dextrous aplomb. When, occasionally, they crash and wipeout, they recover their composure and return to the surface, smiling good humouredly.

For others, school is a very different place. Dipping their toes into the chilly depths of peer group approval is an intimidating experience. More often than not, tsunamis of peer pressure leave them bewildered and broken. Especially when, like today, the other students make obvious their dislike for them. They don't want to sit near them. They don't want to talk to them. They think they're weird. Most of the class seem to feel the same.

How can you integrate this isolated individual?

DOI: 10.4324/9781003440826-24

Avoid saying	Reframe for success
"I want everyone to start being nicer to [student's name]."	"I won't have anyone being left out in this class. I'll be deciding which groups you work in."

Why does this work?

Despite your good intentions, attempting to solve the problem by highlighting the student publicly is likely to lead to further embarrassment and humiliation. The fragile remnants of the ostracised student's confidence can be shattered utterly by a classroom discussion that singles them out.

A better approach is to work on a more inclusive classroom in general terms. This might, for example, involve breaking up influential groups and clamping down immediately on any negative comments about other students by anyone. In the meantime, your work to include a marginalised student can go on behind the scenes, speaking with, and potentially sanctioning, ringleaders outside of the lesson.

Next steps

1. **Speak to kind students privately** – While it may appear that the class are united in their disdain for a student, you will usually find, on reflection, that some students are less vocal than others. A discreet chat with caring students can lead to them offering to help make left out students feel included.

2. **Address specific pastoral concerns** – Immature students will often shun vulnerable students due to pastoral issues, such as poor personal hygiene. Discuss these issues with the relevant staff to remove these barriers to better relationships.

3. **Reflect on your own interactions with the student** – A harsh truth is that students often pick up cues from their teachers. If we find a student difficult and dislikeable, our manner can unintentionally encourage students to follow suit.

The student who rocks back on their chair (#23)

The scenario

Surveying the room, you see students sitting sensibly at their desks. Eyes are focused on you. Pens are hovering above exercise books. And, crucially, chairs are vertical: each chair base is standing upright on four legs.

All chairs, that is, except one. This particular chair teeters at a diagonal. The student slouching on it has tilted the chair backwards so that it now rests on two legs rather than the traditional four. Reclined leisurely, they maintain this tightrope balancing act through a deft combination of the laws of gravity and using their knees under the table as an emergency brake.

How can you get this student to sort out their posture?

DOI: 10.4324/9781003440826-25

Avoid saying

"[Student's name], sit up properly!"

Reframe for success

"A reminder: I expect to see everyone sitting with their chairs on four legs."

Why does this work?

Why do teachers get irritated by students rocking back on two legs of their chair? Well, first, on a practical level, it's a clear health and safety hazard. Teach for long enough and you'll eventually witness a child toppling backwards and hurting themselves or their classmates in the process. Second, although brief movements can help fidgety students gain focus, prolonged chair rocking indicates that the student is more focused on maintaining their balance than paying close attention to learning. It also tends to unsettle those sitting nearby.

As a significantly distracting form of classroom movement, chair rocking is best addressed through subtle gestures or a general restating of expectations rather than publicly highlighting the unwanted behaviour. Chair rockers who are either a) keen to be noticed or b) have taken fidgeting too far are both best dealt with in a depersonalised and non-confrontational manner.

Next steps

1. **Adopt a specific non-verbal signal –** For frequent chair rockers, employ a consistent signal, which is best used discreetly. Place four fingers together then tap them down on your flat palm to show that you want them to right the unbalanced chair.

2. **Give individual gentle reminders –** In addition to gestures, give subtle verbal reminders as they enter the class. You're expecting good focus, including sensible sitting, today.

3. **Use a literary allusion –** Impress them with your knowledge of classic texts by quoting Animal Farm: "Four legs good, two legs bad." They may be perplexed initially but some students will be intrigued to read Orwell's seminal fable.

The class that's noisy when they should be quiet (#24)

The scenario

You've finished explaining a task or discussing a topic. Now, it's time to focus on individual work. To do that successfully, without distraction, requires a purposeful classroom environment. We're talking minimal noise levels or complete silence.

But every time you ask them to work quietly, the noise levels creep up. As soon as the volume reaches a certain level, other students increase their pitch to compete. You shush them and get a momentary respite of silence, yet before long the noise amplifies once more.

What should you do differently?

DOI: 10.4324/9781003440826-26

Avoid saying	Reframe for success
"You're being too noisy. You need to work quietly."	"So we can fully focus, we're going to work in silence."

Why does this work?

The problem with asking students to "work quietly" is that the instruction is vague and unclear. And children will quickly spot the loophole offered by a teacher's imprecise language. How much noise is too much noise? What exactly do you mean by "quiet"? Is talking allowed but shouting forbidden? Are conversations between two students acceptable but those involving four students too much?

These instructions lack the necessary precision to produce an optimal learning environment. Only by setting unambiguous parameters will teachers get the desired noise levels. For example, students should easily understand what "whispering" means. So, if you say "During this task, I only want to hear whispering voices" students will understand your expectations, unlike the vagueness of "I want you to be really quiet."

Next steps

1. **Stay silent as well –** Teachers often fall into the trap of interrupting silent classes with further instructions ("oh, just one more thing…"). Once you've got them silent, resist the urge to interfere!
2. **Allow time for think/pair/share before silent tasks –** Discussing ideas with a talk partner is an important part of problem solving. Giving students plenty of structured opportunities to verbalise their thoughts will make periods of silence seem like less of an imposition.
3. **Justify the need for minimal noise –** Students often believe that they work better when there is background noise, yet research shows that this is not the case. Explain how cognition improves in quieter environments.

The class that complains about your seating plan (#25)

The scenario

It's been a contentious issue right from the start. The class's previous teacher, it would appear, allowed students to sit pretty much where they liked. They speak about your predecessor as if they were cooler than Jack Black's character in *School of Rock*: laid-back, entertaining and not too bothered about whether much work got done.

And then you take over the class. The first lesson, you ask them to line up to be allocated a desk and the rest is… antipathy. Instigating a simple seating plan has led to incessant whingeing. Barely a lesson goes by without someone asking to move or grouching about their nearest neighbour.

How can you stem the flow of near-constant complaints?

DOI: 10.4324/9781003440826-27

Avoid saying

"I've decided to let you sit where you like and see how it goes."

Reframe for success

"I might make some tweaks to my plan over time but where people sit will always be my decision."

Why does this work?

A fundamental part of a teacher's job description is making unpopular decisions for students' own benefit. With very rare exceptions, students struggle to make sensible choices about who would be a good person for them to be seated next to. Frankly, given the opportunity to sit with their friends, most students will be tempted to chat rather than apply themselves to work.

For this reason, we must stay firm in the face of gripes about seating plans. Apart from situations where your seating plan is hindering productivity and creating problems (see #50), there's little need to make changes. But if changes do need to be made, make it clear that you, as the person controlling the room, have been the final arbiter.

Next steps

1. **Take time over seating plans –** Constructing an effective seating plan is an art. Variables like room layout, gender splits and friendship dynamics can add levels of complexity. Scribbling down random names an hour before meeting them doesn't normally end well.
2. **Make up your own mind –** Resist the temptation to ask colleagues about where you should seat students you don't know. Well-meaning advice can sometimes adversely shape your view of students before you've even met them.
3. **Don't be afraid to make immediate changes –** Starting with a clean slate is important. But if it's immediately apparent that some combinations aren't going to work, don't be afraid to say "actually, I think I'm going to put you over here."

The student with poor presentation of work (#26)

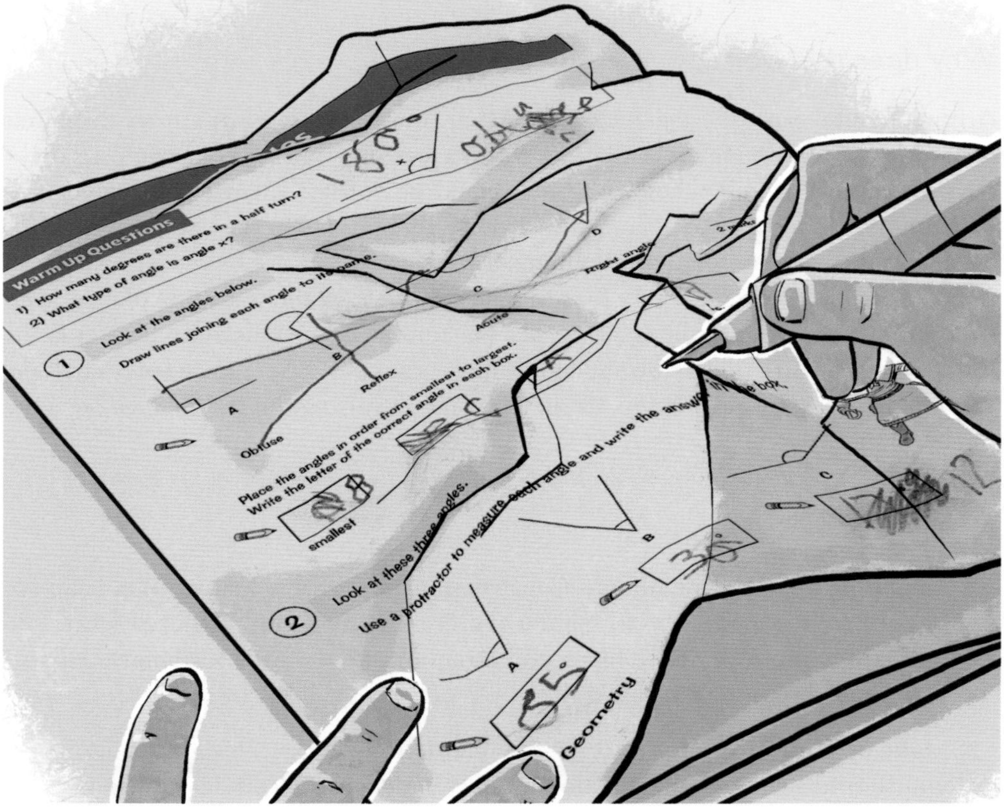

The scenario

Circulating the room and inspecting your students' work, you see a collection of well-organised and well-maintained books. Neat graphs precisely lined using a sharpened pencil. Meticulous diagrams helpfully shaded with a range of colours. Cursive handwriting elegantly transcribed in crisp black ink.

But then you come to a student who displays none of these presentational qualities. Unruled lines are wonkier than cheap flat-pack furniture. Diagrams are about as comprehensible as Avant Garde artwork. Handwriting is scruffier than a landfill tip. Their work is a mess.

How should you deal with poor presentation?

DOI: 10.4324/9781003440826-28

Avoid saying

"This is far too scruffy. Do it again!"

Reframe for success

"I'm concerned that you won't get full credit for your ideas because I'm struggling to understand this work."

Why does this work?

When it comes to the presentation of work, teachers place a high value on neatness. Like smart uniform, tidy presentation is often, understandably, taken as a proxy for student attitude and motivation. Put simply, scruffy presentation is often equated with a lack of care about the work itself.

While there may be some truth in these views, it's important that teachers don't become obsessed about presentation, to the extent that they focus their feedback exclusively on this aspect and ignore the quality of the actual work. Where the presentation is so poor as to obscure meaning, then it absolutely must be addressed. But if enough effort has gone into the work itself, we shouldn't worry about it being aesthetically unappealing. In these circumstances, the focus should be on improving the student, not keeping the page pristine.

Next steps

1. **Show them effective presentation –** We often make assumptions that students are being deliberately messy when they might not fully understand why good presentation is important and how to achieve it. Model this as part of your teaching.

2. **Highlight incomprehensible sections –** If you're really struggling to interpret certain parts of a student's work, identify those passages with a highlighter. This can help careless students appreciate how little of their efforts can be credited.

3. **Is SEND support required? –** Where handwriting is genuinely illegible rather than just scruffy, seek guidance from your SEND coordinator. Time may need to be set aside for handwriting support for students who cannot write clearly.

The class that throws things around the room (#27)

The scenario

Leaning over a desk, explaining something to a student, you feel the weight of a fast-moving projectile as it whizzes six inches over your shoulder. The object – which you quickly recognise as a ballpoint pen – crashes into a display board, ricochets off a desk and skids across the classroom floor.

This is not the first time that something has been launched around the room. Previously, it's been tiny balls of paper, flicked in the direction of a student by another's fingernail. Or a textbook frisbeed along a table before crashing into a student's pencil case, scattering rulers and pens across the floor. It's rude and reckless, and you're furious each time it occurs.

What can you do to stop it happening again?

DOI: 10.4324/9781003440826-29

Avoid saying	Reframe for success
"Who threw that pen? It could've taken someone's eye out!"	"I know which direction that came from. Throwing a pen is dangerous and totally unacceptable. When I discover who threw it there will be consequences."

Why does this work?

Throwing objects in class is disrespectful and hazardous. Naturally, teachers can become enraged by the impertinence and potential harm. Nonetheless, an angry reaction often escalates poor behaviour, amid public arguments about responsibility for the action.

Taking a deep breath before acting helps you take a measured response to an infuriating situation. It's important that the class know that this is a serious issue that will be dealt with. But sometimes you have to accept that you may not get to the bottom of it immediately. Following up after the lesson through private conversations should, however, lead to the identity of the pen-throwing culprit. Then sanctions can be put in place.

Next steps

1. **Avoid whole-class punishments –** In situations where it's unclear who broke the classroom rules, it's tempting to punish the whole class (by keeping them all behind, for example). This is a grave mistake. Innocent students will feel resentment, which could lead to a further breakdown in behaviour standards.

2. **Don't turn your back to some students –** Get into the habit of keeping your body open and frequently moving your attention to areas of the room where you suspect salvos are originating from. Students who feel they are under scrutiny are less likely to throw.

3. **Enlist another pair of eyes –** While you circulate, ask a colleague to spend five minutes observing from a position on the corridor where they can't be seen. They'll be able to spot dodgy stuff you can't see.

The class that is reluctant to respond to feedback (#28)

The scenario

Night after night, to ensure that your students receive detailed written feedback, you spend hours marking. Yet, whenever you hand back work, your comments provoke a minimal response. Some students routinely ignore your feedback, others pay only cursory attention, rushing through their corrections as swiftly as possible. Feedback is seen as a chore, not a gift.

No matter how much you implore them to fix their mistakes and insist that they develop their ideas, they see your feedback as unwelcome and best ignored where possible. It's so frustrating. Unless they respond to your targets, how will they ever improve?

So what can you do to motivate them to act on your feedback?

DOI: 10.4324/9781003440826-30

Avoid saying

"Lots of you didn't listen and made silly errors on your work. Use my comments to make improvements."

Reframe for success

"I'm giving you these comments because I have high expectations of this class. By working on these targets, I know you'll reach my expectations."

Why does this work?

Traditional models position feedback as comments given to a student with the expectancy that they will be automatically acted upon. But to get students responding to feedback, we need to consider the role of motivation in the process.

Students internalise the feedback we give them, thinking about things like our credibility as an expert and whether they trust that we have their best interests at heart. When feedback takes the form of critique – as it inevitably does, at times – we need to reassure students, so that they recognise the benefits of acting on your comments.

Next steps

1. **Make it legible and understandable** – Teachers often mistake students' confusion for a lack of compliance. If they can't read your scrawl, they won't be able to do anything with it! The same goes for verbose targets that cite complex assessment criteria.
2. **Don't make feedback about them** – Focus on improving the work, not critiquing the individual. Instead of "You should have done this," try "Develop your answer by including X and Y."
3. **Be a warm "nit-picker"** – Constantly, but kindly, push all students towards excellence. Expect improvement for even full-mark answers. Communicated in the right way, these apparent minor quibbles signal your sky-high expectations.

The student who misbehaves in your first lesson (#29)

The scenario

Meeting a new class for the first time can be something of a nervy experience. No matter how long you've been in the teaching game, there is always a jittery sensation in the stomach. You compose yourself with a deep breath, greet them and allocate their seats. All seems to be going well.

Within minutes, however, it becomes apparent that one student isn't bothered about getting off to a positive start. Normally, students with a propensity for disruption will wait a few lessons before testing your resolve. With this student, however, it's clear that the traditional honeymoon period is going to be measured in minutes, not hours.

What's the best way of showing this student that you're not to be messed with?

DOI: 10.4324/9781003440826-31

Avoid saying

"[Student's name], I'm going to have my eye on you from now on."

Reframe for success

"You've not made a good first impression. I want you to show me the real, polite, hard-working you."

Why does this work?

When the butterflies start fluttering, we can make rash statements. Our anxieties about making a strong initial impression can lead to overreactions, which can provoke unnecessary conflict at a very early stage of a relationship with a class. As tempting as it might be, public admonishment can create an ill-natured environment from the outset.

A more effective way of dealing with poor behaviour is to set the class off on a task and then have a very quiet word with the wayward student. The message is robust – I'm not happy with how you've behaved so far – but is framed in a positive light. There is the chance for the student to alter your view of them. You are a fair individual who is willing to give second chance because you don't reach fixed opinions of students based on poor first impressions.

Next steps

1. **Don't waste time drawing up rules –** Some teachers spend the first lesson collaborating with the class on a list of behaviour standards. A more effective approach is to provide a brief, simple outline of your behaviour expectations.
2. **Shelve "engaging" lessons –** After a quick behaviour overview, get started with some proper, challenging work. An introductory gimmick-fuelled lesson might be fun, but it could well undermine your credibility as a teacher who expects academic rigour.
3. **Outline a vision for success –** Telling students what you expect in terms of behaviour is vital. But it's also important to talk about what they can expect from you as a teacher. "If you work hard and listen to my feedback, you'll do really well in my class" acts as a powerful incentive.

The class that is unsettled by a new student (#30)

The scenario

A new student saunters through the door. Wearing ripped jeans, classic punk T-shirt and jet-black eyeliner, they exude world weary nonchalance. With smouldering good looks and a copy of The Catcher in the Rye nestled under their arm, they're the rebel archetype epitomised. Assuredly, they slip into an empty chair nearest the coolest kid in class.

This is what happens in the movies. But in a mundane classroom, it's different. Instead of an edgy heartthrob, you're introduced to an awkward and nervous newcomer, desperate to go unnoticed. Meanwhile, the rest of the class snigger and point, exchanging knowing glances like they've just encountered one of the animal kingdom's more exotic creatures.

How can you integrate them and simultaneously settle the class?

DOI: 10.4324/9781003440826-32

Avoid saying

"Right, everyone, this is [insert name], a new student. Make sure you make them feel welcome!"

Reframe for success

"Can you take a seat over there please, [insert name]. Ok, now let's get back on with our work."

Why does this work?

It may be motivated by noble intentions but greeting an anxious new student with a grand introduction is likely to cause further social embarrassment. Thrust into the intense glare of peer scrutiny, the fresh arrival will want to get out of the spotlight as swiftly as possible. Rather than assuaging their nerves, by prolonging the welcome you're prolonging the pain.

For the vast majority of new students on the block, a brisk, low-key introduction to a class will be much appreciated. Giving them time to gradually assimilate is likely to work best. In the meantime, comments from the rest of the class should be treated in the same way as any other off-task chatter. By not making a fuss over the new student, you're signalling to the class that you won't stand for any fuss from them either.

Next steps

1. **Choose a sympathetic talk partner** – Selecting an appropriate spot on your seating plan is an essential first move. Placing them next to a friendly and industrious student will ease them into the group and help to avoid feelings of isolation.

2. **Be clear about the classroom culture** – Not knowing what to expect from a teacher can lead to new students making mortifying gaffes, leading to mockery by classmates. Ensure fresh arrivals get a quick sense of how things work in your room.

3. **Ask questions you know they can answer** – Cold call can put students on the spot before they've had time to settle. Ensure you ask questions on topics that new students have had the opportunity to learn, to avoid possible embarrassment.

The student who makes deliberately distracting noises (#31)

The scenario

A hushed, anticipatory silence falls on the auditorium. This most eagerly awaited recital will feature a once-in-a-generation talent, a virtuoso soloist playing one of the finest concertos in the history of music. Stretching their fingers, puffing out their cheeks, then picking up their priceless instrument, they begin. It starts with a brisk allegro then morphs skilfully into the warmth of the darting melodic lines.

Back in the real world of the classroom, the silence is disturbed by something else. Rather than a world-class flautist, you have the unpleasant pitched whistle of a Biro lid, played surreptitiously by a misbehaving student. The identity of the person making this ear-piercing racket is as yet unclear. But some of the audience are enjoying the entertainment.

As classroom conductor, how can you muzzle this unwanted musician?

DOI: 10.4324/9781003440826-33

Avoid saying

"Whoever's making that annoying noise needs to stop it now."

Reframe for success

"As we're working in silence, I shouldn't be hearing any noise now."

Why does this work?

When students make deliberately irritating noises, they are looking to provoke a reaction. The first reaction they wish to provoke is from you. An angry or exasperated outburst will add to the fun. The second thing they want to happen is for other anonymous whistlers to join in. After all, a discordant duet is even more enjoyable than an individual performance.

Your general reminder about silence then serves two purposes: a) it disguises your annoyance, which robs the disruptive noisemaker of the pleasure of seeing you rattled, and b) it buys you time to locate the source of the whistling. By standing strategically and looking for students with pens (or other objects) near mouths, you should be able to spot the culprit and dish out the usual sanction for deliberate disruption of a lesson.

Next steps

1. **Check the SEND register** – Some students make involuntary noises and movements due to medical conditions such as Tourette's. Avoid embarrassing accusations by keeping fully up to date with the SEND details of the students you teach.

2. **Remove access to "musical instruments"** – Once you've identified students who like to make noise in this way, ensure they put away pen tops and the like during your lessons. Other instruments, like twanged rubber bands or shatter-proof rulers need to be binned or confined to pencil cases.

3. **Treat troublesome coughs** – Mysteriously theatrical coughs also cause issues during quiet periods of work. To begin with, provide a drink of water to rule out a dry throat and then raise the problem with parents. Might a trip to the doctors be necessary?

The student who doesn't care about detentions (#32)

The scenario

The student's behaviour has fallen well short of what you expect. Whether it's disruption in class, lateness, lack of equipment or yet another missed homework deadline, you're not impressed by their conduct. As a result, you decide to hand out a detention. Let's see how they like it when you take back some of their precious social time!

But when you inform the young miscreant of their punishment, they display complete indifference. Reaching for their planner, they shake their head and give a nonchalant shrug of the shoulders. Like an in-demand plumber flicking through a packed diary, they don't have space to fit you in any time soon.

What's your next move?

 DOI: 10.4324/9781003440826-34

Avoid saying	Reframe for success
"In that case, I'll book you in for a detention in three weeks' time."	"Ok, you can expect to hear from me shortly with a different sanction."

Why does this work?

In a school where the behaviour policy states that teachers are responsible for running their own detentions, some students can rack up an inordinate number of detentions. Consequently, detention slots can fill up rather quickly for certain students. Playing teachers off against one another, these students will often take great delight in not being able to attend detentions at your preferred time.

When students don't see a detention as a deterrent, there's little point in handing them out for the sake of it. A useful question to ask yourself is *what does this student not want me to do in these circumstances?* It might be arranging for them to spend your next lesson working in isolation with a senior leader. It might be missing out on a reward of some kind. Thinking creatively can help disrupt the sense that they are impervious to consequences.

Next steps

1. **Lobby for whole-school approaches –** Managing detentions in this way isn't effective or sustainable in terms of workload or impact. Press senior colleagues for a centralised solution to detentions.

2. **Ensure detentions aren't enjoyable –** If you do have to run your own detentions in the long-term, make sure they are silent sessions where students are expected to work hard.

3. **Discuss strategies with colleagues –** Some of the other teachers at your school may have better ways of dealing with students who pick up detentions. Discuss how they manage this balance and borrow their helpful ideas.

The class that claims your sanctions are unfair (#33)

The scenario

We've got massive news coming from today's big grudge match. Let's go to Alan, our pitch side reporter, for an update… Unbelievable scenes here, Kelly. There's been a few big decisions gone against the home team and the atmosphere has quickly turned sour. The referee has been surrounded by a handful of furious players, challenging several huge calls. Naturally the crowd have gone bananas; objects have been thrown onto the pitch and chants of "You're not fit to referee" fill the air.

You're not an actual referee. And this isn't a sports stadium. But with this class, whenever you make key calls about behaviour management, it sometimes feels like it. Roars of protest. Decisions constantly questioned. Partisan peers chipping in unhelpfully.

How can you tackle behaviour and maintain control of the class?

DOI: 10.4324/9781003440826-35

Avoid saying	Reframe for success
"My decisions are final. I don't care what you all think."	"If I get things wrong, I will happily change my mind. But my expectations are really clear. Let me remind the class what behaviours I need to see."

Why does this work?

Like all other humans, teachers sometimes make mistakes. As such, it's always worth buying yourself a bit of time to think about whether you made the right call. A rigid refusal to perform a U-turn can lead to a breakdown in teacher/class relationships. An unwillingness to budge leads to a deterioration in behaviour, fuelled by feelings of injustice.

Of course, with some classes, perfectly reasonable decisions are challenged, purely down to students refusing to accept responsibility for their actions. Being able to quickly evaluate the fairness of our sanctions is an important skill for any teacher. Once we're certain that we've made the right call, we can stand firm behind our decisions. Our calls might not be popular, but a general reminder of precise expectations will help quell a potentially mutinous class.

Next steps

1. **Don't get into long debates –** Be prepared to offer a brief explanation of why a sanction has been given but don't become tangled up in lengthy arguments. If they want a more detailed discussion, that can take place during their social time.

2. **Avoid scattergun escalations –** Frustrated by students arguing back, teachers often fire off multiple warnings in retaliation. Taking a calming deep breath when irritated should help keep these scattergun sanctions to a minimum.

3. **Don't hand out punishments with glee –** When sanctions are given, they are best delivered with a tone of reluctance. A wise teacher is willing to use sanctions when necessary but would much rather not need to dole them out in the first place.

The class that talks over you (#34)

The scenario

You're in the zone. The idea you're explaining is difficult to grasp, but you're doing a fine job of making the complex accessible. You've given this explanation many times before, but this is the first time that you're really nailing it. It's taken a couple of minutes of talk, but you know it's vital that they understand this key point.

Just as you reach the crux of your highly structured elaboration, you look around and see a few groups of students chatting. Deep in conversation, these groups have obviously stopped listening to you and, to your great vexation, have chosen to have their own cosy off-task discussions instead. This kind of thing is happening all the time.

What's the best way to deal with this common problem?

DOI: 10.4324/9781003440826-36

Avoid saying

"Stop talking while I'm talking. It's so rude!"

Reframe for success

"A reminder that when I'm speaking, nobody else speaks."

Why does this work?

Improving the listening habits of a class like this takes time. Some students will need frequent reminders of your expectations before they break their off-task chatter habit. Immediately highlighting poor behaviour through an angry, public scolding can lead to a backlash and an escalation of the unwanted behaviour.

Instead, give a calm, generalised reminder of what students need to do while you're speaking. This is non-negotiable and easy to understand. If, despite your pre-warning reminder, students continue to chat, then you will, of course, hand out appropriate sanctions. But this depersonalised, unambiguous and non-confrontational stance usually leads to quieter classes quicker than sanctions alone. It embodies a firm but fair approach.

Next steps

1. ***Never* allow students to talk over you** – As a teacher, this rule must be immutable. At no point should you continue speaking while students are having their own conversation. Fail to hold this line and you'll have a career full of disrupted lessons.

2. **Give a look to silence them** – Disapproving eye contact (#98) is a major weapon in a teacher's behaviour arsenal. Deploy this first before stopping your flow to restate your expectations.

3. **Tweak your seating plan** – Refreshing your seating plan can help to break up chatty pairs and groups. It may take a few versions before you manage to disperse talkative students.

The student who says your lessons are boring (#35)

The scenario

You spend ages planning your lessons. Hours of research to make sure your subject knowledge is fully up-to-date. Hours creating resources that are accessible and visually appealing. Hours thinking about the key knowledge students need to know and how best to impart it.

And then one day during class, a student sighs theatrically and announces that "this lesson is *boring*". It's loud enough to be audible to the rest of the class. It's quite rude and, understandably, you're annoyed by this statement.

How should you respond when a student accuses you of being a tedious teacher?

DOI: 10.4324/9781003440826-37

Avoid saying

"I don't care if you think it's boring; you still need to know it for your exams."

Reframe for success

"You might feel like that now but I'm confident that if you give this subject your best, you'll find it more enjoyable eventually."

Why does this work?

This type of comment feels very personal. And it's difficult – especially when you work so hard to plan and deliver effective lessons – not to take it to heart. But in the vast majority of cases this kind of comment reflects more on the students' sense of self-worth than the quality of your pedagogy.

By rising above the slur apparently directed at you, you're able to reframe the discussion so that the focus is on their effort and motivation rather than your teaching. It may be tempting to resort to sarcasm and tell them that it might be boring, but they will just need to lump it. But that kind of approach fails to take into account that students often need to feel successful before they start to enjoy a topic.

Next steps

1. **Only allow them one free pass** – Despite the provocation, you've dealt with this calmly and assuredly. But if the student uses this expression again, the rudeness will warrant a robust sanction.
2. **Maintain your enthusiasm for all topics you teach** – When teachers apologise for certain "dry" topics it can demotivate students further. Avoid describing your least favourite topics as "a bit dull."
3. **Create opportunities for the student to taste success** – Rudeness like this can be a façade that attempts to hide a lack of confidence. Provide a greater range of scaffolding for this student and they're more likely to start enjoying the subject.

The student who struggles to deal with frustration (#36)

The scenario

You're handing back test papers. Marking them, you could sense your students' perspiration levels. Everyone tried their best. But, unfortunately, not everyone did well. The papers – featuring a prominent percentage in the top right-hand corner, scrawled in a strident crimson ink – are doled out.

As tests land on desks, some are met with outbursts of pleasure, some with the silence of disappointment. One student, however, is obviously unimpressed. Angry with the result, with the topic, with you, perhaps with the world itself, this student has screwed their paper up and has launched it into a nearby waste basket.

How should you deal with this sudden outburst?

DOI: 10.4324/9781003440826-38

Avoid saying	Reframe for success
"That's unacceptable behaviour. I'm giving you a warning."	"I'm pleased to see you care so much about doing well. But you need to understand that struggle is an essential part of success."

Why does this work?

Learning is hard work. We know this, right? Apart from a tiny minority who excel intuitively at maths, English and pretty much everything else, we all have our struggles along the way. When we become expert at a subject, we can forget the innumerable difficulties we faced along the way. We might not have binned our papers, or flung our textbooks across the desk, but there will have been times when we felt like doing so.

So instead of punishing these temper flares, we should help students see the bigger picture. First, frustration is a sign that they are challenging themselves with more complex work. Stick with it, and they'll get the deep satisfaction that comes with doing well despite finding things hard. Reframing struggle as an integral component of success helps students rationalise their feelings of dismay at poor results along the path to good outcomes.

Next steps

1. **Stop talking about marks and grades** – Help lower the stakes by reducing talk about marks and grades. A reassuring message for students is "work hard on the feedback I've given you and, eventually, the marks will take care of themselves."

2. **Celebrate perseverance** – Praise the class when they continue to make progress despite finding work difficult: "I know this is a tricky task, but I'm really pleased that you've stuck with it and are getting there."

3. **Pre-empt disappointment before giving back results** – Placing the test into context, by reinforcing the complexity of tasks for example, can help students cope better with the frustration of poor performance.

The class that is reluctant to answer questions (#37)

The scenario

A silent classroom is often a productive classroom. But sometimes silence can be painful and indicative of students switching off. Each time you pose questions you see the same pattern of behaviour. Some students avoid eye contact and duck down their heads, attempting to avoid having to respond to your questions.

Others, meanwhile, are keen to thrust themselves forward, demonstrating their understanding of the subject with relative ease. Every time you put forward a question, they extend their arms and give an expectant look, pleading with you to pick them once more.

How can you increase participation from your reluctant students?

DOI: 10.4324/9781003440826-39

Avoid saying

"Does anyone know the answer?"

Reframe for success

"So that I can hear all your ideas, I'll be asking everyone questions. Let's start with..."

Why does this work?

In a classroom where the cleverest or most enthusiastic students respond to the bulk of questions, other students will quickly realise that they can get away with less hard thinking. Once they recognise that a teacher is throwing out questions to anyone who fancies answering them, they'll down metaphorical tools and drift off, safe in the knowledge that they are unlikely to be called upon.

Yet, in a classroom where cold call is the default questioning strategy, students will come to realise that there is no hiding place and that deeper thinking is obligatory. By reminding students that their thoughts are equally important, and by gently insisting on contributions from all, you can significantly increase both answering and thinking.

Next steps

1. **Build the confidence of introverts –** To help shy students, give them discreet notice about questions you will ask them. Alternatively, to begin with, ask them questions to which they'll definitely know the correct answer.

2. **Move between cold call and hands up –** Sticking to cold call too rigidly can backfire. Very tricky questions work better if you revert to hands up and ask for volunteers.

3. **Use names at the end of questions –** When using cold call, it's still possible to inadvertently signal to the class that they can take a mental break. To increase whole class thinking time, instead of saying the student's name first, save the name for the end of the question.

The class that is reluctant to edit and improve work (#38)

The scenario

Rushed, lacking in detail and riddled with mistakes. Whether it's in class or when marking books you've collected in, the work you see is unimpressive. Students seem to be doing the absolute minimum to meet the demands of the task. They fill in the boxes, answer the questions and write the requisite number of paragraphs. But they don't go any further.

What you view as first drafts are seen by students as complete pieces of work. Symbolic of their general disdain for extended writing, your tasks are seen as a means to an end, to be finished briskly without any need for revision. It's holding back their progress and it's driving you mad.

How can you release their inner editor?

DOI: 10.4324/9781003440826-40

Avoid saying

"Do your edits now or you'll be doing them in detention."

Reframe for success

"The first thing we write is rarely our best work. If we're going to make our work more impressive, there's always room for improvement."

Why does this work?

It can be extremely irritating when students aren't keen on improving their work. It smacks of laziness and implies that they are completing work quickly so that they can have a breather before the next task. It suggests a "that'll do" attitude towards their learning. While this may be the case for some students, it's more likely that they have yet to grasp the huge benefits of editing work. And sanctions are unlikely to disrupt this mindset.

By highlighting the gains made by students who go beyond the first draft, it's possible to shift the classroom culture to one of striving for continual improvement. Using before and after pieces – especially when done live during a lesson – emphasises the profound differences that a critical appraisal of our work can bring. Motivating them to make amendments is a much more fruitful approach in the long run.

Next steps

1. **Show them how to edit –** Students often have surprisingly little idea what "editing" means. Talk them through the precise weaknesses of your exemplars and show exactly how to make changes for the better.

2. **Give specific examples –** Vague feedback, like "use better vocab" or "write more sophisticated sentences" is unlikely to help. Use examples that they can adapt in their own work. Integrate these into your models as well.

3. **Provide simple checklists –** Before students submit work, ask them to tick off straightforward criteria based on your specific examples. Keep this list accessible and brief to avoid cognitive overload.

The student who makes misogynistic comments (#39)

The scenario

You get on well with the male students you teach. Your relationships with boys are solid. They know you care about them and expect them to do well. You set firm but fair boundaries; there's a feeling of mutual respect in your classroom.

Recently, however, you've become concerned about one boy's behaviour. Silly comments about real men being physically strong. Lame jokes about women being rubbish drivers. Until now, you've taken a low-key approach. Today, however, they completely overstepped the line. They said women are inferior to men and that a woman's place is in the kitchen.

How should you respond to this misogynistic behaviour?

DOI: 10.4324/9781003440826-41

Avoid saying	**Reframe for success**
"I'm putting you in detention with [female SLT member]. I'd like to see you say that to her!"	"What makes you say that? Do you really believe that?"

Why does this work?

Misogynistic comments are deeply offensive, especially for female teachers. But before giving immediate sanctions, it's worth asking questions to place derogatory statements in context. Is this something that they really believe or is it an immature provocation, just to get a reaction? If they apologise, a mindless comment can lead to a powerful learning opportunity.

One possible explanation for the misogynistic comments is that they have fallen under the sway of a social media influencer who espouses outrageous beliefs as part of their online persona. If, after further clarification, they stand by their comments then serious consequences become absolutely necessary, as well as a safeguarding referral to address their extreme views. Female teachers should not have to endure personal insults.

Next steps

1. **Avoid silencing boys –** Social media influencers claim they are being cancelled for "speaking the truth". If we shut down debate immediately, male students are likely to believe this myth. Discussion may be difficult but, at some point, it's essential.

2. **Is now the time for a debate? –** If you're understandably upset by a student's comments, however, you might want to delay discussing the issues. Taking time to calm down before addressing the matter will help you educate the student in a rational way.

3. **Take ownership of further sanctions –** If, for example, a boy is removed from a female teacher's class by a male colleague, it's important that it doesn't appear that the teacher is being "rescued." If you find yourself in this situation, insist on being involved when sanctions are given.

The student who keeps turning round in their chair (#40)

The scenario

Like a fairground Waltzer, they enjoy nothing more than a good spin. During explanation, they turn around. During instructions they turn around. During independent work they turn around. It's not much of an exaggeration to say that you're more familiar with the back of their head than their facial appearance.

You've experimented with different seating plans. But placing them in different locations hasn't made any difference. You've considered sticking them at the back of the room, so the only thing they will be able to interact with if they spin round is the wall. Ultimately, however, you prefer to sit this student near the front, under your proverbial nose.

So how can you get them to face the right way?

DOI: 10.4324/9781003440826-42

Avoid saying

"[Student's name], turn around!"

Reframe for success

"Everyone facing the front … I'm still waiting for some of you to be looking this way."

Why does this work?

Students who like to turn around in their seats usually do so for one of two reasons. First, they like chatting during lessons and prefer talking to those behind them over those sitting beside them. Second, they wish to demonstrate to the rest of the class that they aren't following the rules. What could be more rebellious than not looking at the person who is trying to educate them?

When a teacher draws repeated attention to the student doing a 180-degree turn, therefore, they amplify the student's act of rebellion. For this reason, a depersonalised approach is essential. By using generalised reminders – repeated after a pause, then a long wait, if necessary – the student is deprived of the oxygen of publicity.

Next steps

1. **Use a non-verbal signal** – The turnaround hand gesture (#93) is a vital component in a teacher's behaviour management toolbox. You'll find it has a much higher success rate than naming the student who is facing the wrong way.
2. **Give discreet praise for compliance** – At the end of lessons, tell the student you're impressed that they're turning around less frequently and have noticed an improvement in their work as a result. You'll be even more impressed when they stop doing it completely.
3. **Alter your position during independent work** – When students are doing extended silent work, go stand at the back of the room occasionally. The student will be surprised to see you and will usually perform a swift U-turn and get back to their work.

The class that is unsettled by the presence of a wasp (#41)

The scenario

Once upon a time, in a classroom far away, a teacher sat working at a cluttered desk while their students studied diligently. It was a beautiful day in late summer. The only sound was the soothing chirrup of birds in nearby trees and the occasional flap of a venetian blind swaying gently in the breeze from open windows.

Suddenly, a faint droning noise disturbed the silence. Before the poor teacher knew what was happening a commotion erupted: chairs scraped across the floor; a child's high-pitched scream; an exodus from the desks by the window. The hapless teacher saw that a beastly wasp had flown into the room!

How could the teacher stop the lesson being ruined by this untimely insect invasion?

DOI: 10.4324/9781003440826-43

Avoid saying	Reframe for success
"Sit back down and get on with your work! It's only a little."	"Everyone try to stay calm while I coax it back out of the window."

Why does this work?

In this context, you need to be realistic and accept that normal rules do not apply. Given the rare opportunity of watching their newspaper-wielding teacher do battle with a sugar-fuelled black and yellow hooligan, what student is going to be able to carry on with their work?

We should always strive for maximum concentration levels in lessons. But in this instance, we might as well shrug our shoulders, admit defeat and accept that the next few minutes of pest control will render futile all attempts to keep the lesson moving along. The only question now is how quickly you – or a brave but sensible nominated substitute – can encourage the demented marauder to clear off before you slam the window shut.

Next steps

1. **Prepare for other intrusions –** Stinging insects may be the teacher's nemesis, but they are by no means the only major distraction. Trying to give instructions to the backdrop of a leaf blower or contractor's drill is also pointless.

2. **Pay close attention to the weather forecast –** Climatic conditions can sometimes inflict even more havoc on an unexpecting educator. Torrential rain, hail, snow and, especially, strong winds have wrecked many an impeccably planned lesson.

3. **Use the situation as a learning opportunity –** If you can't beat them, consider joining them. Abandon your activity and ask them to conduct a subject-specific task: a poem about snow, a quiz on types of precipitation, a graph on their least favourite insects, etc.

The student who shouts at you (#42)

The scenario

The tension in the room is palpable. Things have been escalating for a while now. Each time you ask a specific student to do something – or indeed to stop doing something – the response has been one of increasing belligerence. A deep sigh became a muttered grumble. A muttered grumble became a contemptuous look. A contemptuous look became a raw-throated outburst.

You made a seemingly mundane request for them to turn around and get on with their work. And now they're screaming at you in front of the rest of the class. Shocked into silence by the ferocity of this guttural howl, the class sits, mouths open, awaiting your response.

What's your next move?

DOI: 10.4324/9781003440826-44

Avoid saying

"How dare you raise your voice at me!"

Reframe for success

"I'm not shouting at you, so I'm not sure why you're shouting at me."

Why does this work?

Occasionally, students get the feeling that we've got it in for them. They think our greatest joy in life comes from harassing and picking on them. As a result of this perceived prodding and poking, they sometimes snap. While there are things we can do to manage this sense of injustice (see #8), sometimes we find ourselves on the receiving end of a frustrated scream.

In these circumstances, turning down the temperature is the only effective form of action. Shouting back at a shouting student will only provoke more shouting. Before you know it, you'll be embroiled in a full-scale slanging match, worthy of any soap opera. By calmly reminding the student that you aren't seeking conflict, you can reduce the emotional heat before you consider an appropriate consequence for the loss of temper.

Next steps

1. **Avoid yelling in class** – Shouting is ineffective and damaging to relationships with students. What's more, it soon loses its impact and becomes viewed as background noise by students. As soon as you shout, you've lost your cool and their respect.

2. **Intervene before things come to a head** – When a student shows repeated signs of frustration at your reprimands, arrange an informal meeting with a pastoral lead. Listen to their grievances but explain why your expectations must be followed.

3. **Use quiet rebukes when necessary** – Public rebukes can cause embarrassment and resentment. Whenever possible, manage poor behaviour in a subtle way. This might involve whispering expectations in the student's ear or taking them outside for a quick reminder of what behaviour modifications you need to see.

The student who mocks your attempts at humour (#43)

The scenario

Did you hear the one about the constipated mathematician? He had to work it out with a pencil! What's a six-sided shape called? Yes, it's a hexagon. And a five-sided shape? Yes, that's right, it's a pentagon? But what about a no-sided shape? That's got you, hasn't it? Well, it's just called a "gon"! Gon. No sides. Gone. Geddit?! Ha ha ha ha ha!

If the truth be told, a little part of you always fancied becoming a stand-up comedian. You're hilarious. Even if you do say so yourself. Plenty of kids have giggled at your jokes during your teaching career, though. But this student doesn't laugh at all. Not even in a pretend wincing, I'm smiling because that's terrible kind of way. They're actually rude about your jokes.

How should you deal with this unexpected heckler?

DOI: 10.4324/9781003440826-45

Avoid saying

"I'm just trying to lighten the atmosphere. Are your jokes any better?"

Reframe for success

"I know, that was a dreadful joke. Still, I did get a few laughs."

Why does this work?

Humour can help cement positive relationships with students. But it can also backfire. While most students respond to a humorous interlude with good grace and polite appreciation, others can find it irritating. Perhaps they're not in the mood? Perhaps they'd rather just get on with learning? Perhaps – no, surely not – you're just not that funny. Behaving in a defensive and argumentative way can cause further fractures in your relationships with students.

For this reason, when dealing with a grumpy audience member... sorry, student... self-deprecation is the biggest weapon in your comedic arsenal. Head off any complaints about the quality of your jokes by acknowledging their dubious quality first. And if a student still doesn't warm to your sub-standard gags, maybe ration them from now on.

Next steps

1. **Focus on being respected, not being liked** – Developing positive relationships with students is very important. Courting popularity, however, should not be your aim. Being seen as firm and fair is far more important than being seen as cool and funny.

2. **Try not to take things personally** – When students mock your jokes, mannerisms and other quirks, it's easy to take things to heart. These things are rarely about you as an individual though. Sometimes, children are just being rebellious or immature; remember that these apparent slights usually say more about them than about you.

3. **Avoid joking during complex explanations** – The beauty of humour is that we remember good jokes. The downside of humour is that we might remember good jokes at the expense of the important topic we were meant to be learning.

The class that encourages you to digress to avoid work (#44)

The scenario

From the very beginning, you've felt relaxed with the class. Instructions are followed. Work is completed. Behaviour is very good. The atmosphere in the class is purposeful but fun. As a result, you find yourself loosening the reins at times. Drifting away from the narrow focus of drier topics, you use anecdotes and digressions to enliven things further.

The class responds very well to this combination of personal warmth and intellectual curiosity. There's only one real issue. Some of the class have noticed your willingness to take the more scenic route on occasion. Sensing that your impromptu facts and stories can delay "real work" for a while, they prompt you to do this at each opportunity.

How should you respond to their efforts to divert from the lesson aims?

DOI: 10.4324/9781003440826-46

Avoid saying	Reframe for success
"We don't have time for that now."	"Let's focus on what we're doing, and we'll see if there's time to come back to that later."

Why does this work?

As behaviour problems go, this is a relatively nice problem to have. Your rapport with the class is strong, and they obviously enjoy listening to your fascinating tales and footnotes. Having piqued their interest, you don't want to quash their enthusiasm by blocking off potentially stimulating detours.

Nonetheless, you still need to avoid them taking advantage of you. In these circumstances, therefore, make it clear that you welcome the chance to digress, but only if the main thrust of the lesson is covered. Where students just want to distract, this approach can delay the deviation indefinitely. Where students are genuinely keen to hear more, it acts as a motivation to work hard.

Next steps

1. **Think carefully about what you share –** Storytelling is an integral part of effective teaching but when it comes to anecdotes, reflect carefully on the amount of personal information you want to divulge. Discussing your dislike of sprouts is far less controversial, for example, than talking about topics like political beliefs.

2. **Consider the learning benefits –** Seemingly irrelevant digressions can sometimes have powerful benefits. Random discussions about the etymology of words or the lives of famous scientists can spark students' imaginations in an unexpected way.

3. **Set aside time for fun and wonder –** Squeezing lots of learning out of lesson time is important. But sometimes it's worthwhile ditching the lesson plan for the last five minutes. Chatting about a job you used to have, or that time you met a celebrity, can spark interesting discussions.

The class that you really dislike teaching (#45)

The scenario

As they step through the door, apprehension takes a grip of your innards. Shoulders tighten. Armpits moisten. Your heartbeat quickens. Hesitation and uncertainty solidifies into anxiety and dread. They've already entered the hall of infamy as Least Favourite Class Ever.

Everything you've tried so far has ended in abject failure. If anything, they seem to be getting worse. Sanctions deflect off them as if they're shrouded by an invisible forcefield of apathy. They're immune to praise and rewards. The mere mention of the class's name triggers feelings of despair. Put simply, you can't stand this class.

How should you manage these feelings?

DOI: 10.4324/9781003440826-47

Avoid saying

"I've had just about enough of this class."

Reframe for success

"I normally love teaching this class. But I'm not happy with some of the behaviour I'm seeing."

Why does this work?

Once a class gets the sense that a teacher dislikes them, their behaviour invariably deteriorates further. A lack of affection – whether it's justified or not – has a predictably dire impact on the self-concept of young people. Subtle cues and hints of dislike cause more issues. Open acknowledgements of distaste lead to irreparable relationship breakdowns.

In this situation you must bury your personal feelings behind an impenetrable veneer of professionalism. In other words, you have to learn to love – or at least give a good impression of loving – the thing you strongly dislike. Never has the cliché "fake it till you make it" been more apt. Smile and tell them you enjoy teaching them and they'll start to believe you. Over time, as their behaviour improves, you might come to believe it yourself!

Next steps

1. **Minimise opportunities for poor behaviour –** Teachers can be tempted to plan "engaging" activities in an effort to pacify poorly behaved classes. Resist this temptation, prioritising silent individual work until behaviour improves.
2. **Discuss the class with trusted colleagues –** Teachers who also teach the class, or have taught them before, may have sensible advice to help manage their behaviour. If not, knowing that you're not alone in this situation can be reassuring in itself. If you continue to struggle, insist on further SLT support.
3. **Treat each day as a fresh start –** Carrying over resentment from the previous day will only exacerbate the negativity in the room. Avoiding grudges is a central part of moving forward. Project warmth as they enter the class but offer firm reminders of your expectations moving forward.

The student who rolls their eyes at you (#46)

The scenario

Each time you make a lame joke, it happens. Each time you remind students of a disliked rule, it happens. Each time you tell a personal anecdote, it happens. In fact, there are few occasions when you say something to the class, and it doesn't happen. This student is clearly unimpressed with (a) your teaching and (b) every other thing about you.

As facial gestures go, it's about as subtle as a brick through a window. The unmistakable revolving eyeballs, accompanied with a dismissive tilt of the head. As predictable as a Wednesday following a Tuesday, your words are habitually followed by this student rolling their eyes with an Oscar-worthy flourish.

What should you do about these contemptuous expressions?

DOI: 10.4324/9781003440826-48

Avoid saying

"Give me that look one more time and you're out!"

Reframe for success

"So, what I'd like us to do now is..."

Why does this work?

Teaching isn't a popularity contest. To paraphrase the cliché, you can please some of your students all of the time but you can't please a few of your students any of the time. And nor should you attempt to. Making unpopular decisions for the benefit of students is a fundamental part of a teacher's job. Some won't appreciate your efforts and will make this evident through dismissive gestures. But, as long as they comply, who cares?

Getting into a confrontation with students over rude facial expressions is unlikely to modify their behaviour. No matter how frustrating you find their sneering disdain, it's better to just ignore it. As long as it doesn't spill over into audible defiance or a refusal to work then just... let it go. The chances are they'll eventually grow tired of the unrewarded effort of contorting their facial muscles and simply stop doing it.

Next steps

1. **Remain utterly professional –** With students who are angling for conflict, it's important to display excessive politeness. Thank the class for keeping their eyes on you as you talk from the front. This will seriously annoy the eye-roller.
2. **Maintain your sense of humour –** Wannabe stand-up comedians can make tiresome teachers. But the odd self-deprecating gag is helpful for building a rapport with a class. Make a show of laughing when they scorn your rubbish humour. This show of humility will defuse the eyeroller's visual bombs.
3. **Don't dodge them during questioning –** You might be tempted to ignore this derisive individual while cold calling. This is a mistake. Engage them fully during questioning and ensure you are complimentary about impressive responses.

The student who ignores your instructions (#47)

The scenario

Have you become invisible? It would appear so. From the student's perspective you seem to have vanished, perhaps spontaneously combusting after too many breaktime coffees. You give the class instructions. They comply. All except one. This student prefers to do their own thing, pretending you're an imaginary teacher who doesn't exist.

Today was an infuriating example. You asked the class to end their discussion, turn and face the front. Everyone conformed apart from the student who acts like you're inaudible as well as invisible. Carrying on talking to another student, they acted as if no instructions had been given. Rebukes make little difference: they carry on as if nothing has been said.

How can you get them to do as they're told?

DOI: 10.4324/9781003440826-49

Avoid saying

"[Student's name], can you please just do what you've been asked?"

Reframe for success

"I'm still waiting for some of you to follow my instructions. I'm not prepared to wait much longer."

Why does this work?

Having instructions routinely ignored by a student can cause serious frustration. And that frustration can understandably manifest itself in repeated public scolding of the student. This often takes the form of a passive aggressive rhetorical question, which is intended to sound authoritative, but usually sounds like a desperate plea from a worn-down teacher.

Students tend not to be incentivised to improve their behaviour after a public telling off. Those who behave in this way are usually keen to be noticed by peers. And using their name draws attention to them, bringing them kudos via public admonishment. Far better to offer general reminders about your expectations. Then wait until they look your way. If this doesn't work, a warning should be given as discreetly as possible. Eventually, they will grasp that you won't continue until all instructions are followed.

Next steps

1. **Pluralise behaviour expectations** – Even when it's just one student causing issues, use language that doesn't single them out for negative attention. Using vague quantifiers like "some" or "a few" prevents it from seeming like a head-to-head battle.

2. **Notice good behaviour anonymously** – Narrating the positives uses the power of belonging to persuade disruptive students to comply. Done anonymously, it avoids embarrassing students who might not want their obedience publicised.

3. **Use opportunities to make positive calls home** – Positive phone calls home can have a lasting impact on student behaviour. They must be fully deserved, of course. Seize the chance to make congratulatory calls after sustained behaviour improvements.

The class that is unsettled by classroom visitors (#48)

The scenario

A cramped, poorly ventilated classroom, 15 minutes before lunchtime. The STUDENTS *are concentrating on their work. The* TEACHER *is reclined at a desk, presumably responding to emails. The only discernible noise is the faint buzzing of the overhead projector.*

HEADTEACHER:	(*opening the door and coming in*): And as you can see, we run a tight ship here. Our emphasis is on hard work and rigid discipline.
VISITOR:	(*Following through the door and speaking loudly*): Very impressi–
The STUDENTS:	lose focus instantly. Noise levels rocket. The TEACHER leaps out of their chair, as if realising they've been sitting on a drawing pin, then shushes venomously at the class.

How can you stop this scene playing out in your classroom?

DOI: 10.4324/9781003440826-50

Avoid saying

"Just ignore our visitors, please."

Reframe for success

"This class can get a bit excited when we have visitors. I'm going to ask them to show you their usual brilliant focus now."

Why does this work?

Asking students to pretend visitors aren't there is futile. It's the equivalent of asking them to ignore a settling snowstorm or 90 decibel lawnmower outside the classroom window. Also, it will strike some visitors as rude; they may wish to engage with the students and talk with them about their learning. This won't be possible if they've been told to blank visitors.

A more fruitful strategy is to acknowledge their excitement when a visitor arrives. Next, follow this with an explicit compliment and an implicit nudge to improve concentration levels. By doing this, you'll find that they are encouraged to show off their best side to visitors. The combination of flattery and a reminder of normal high standards usually works.

Next steps

1. **Ask to be notified in advance –** Having lots of visitors to your room is usually a sign that you're a good teacher; school leaders normally cherry-pick where they take visitors. But knowing when they're coming will mean that you can prepare them for the interruption and help keep them settled.
2. **Train them to interact helpfully –** Students can often become flustered or monosyllabic when unused to responding to visitor's questions. Discuss how to do this and reinforce this through your own communication with other adults.
3. **Get ready for the post-visit eruption –** When students exert themselves putting on a good show for visitors, there is often a short outburst after they leave the room. Prepare yourself for this and allow them a brief moment to regain their focus.

The class that talks over each other (#49)

The scenario

Gradually, following lots of reminders, you've developed a classroom culture where students listen while you're talking. Previously your talk would be punctuated with students talking over you. Now, thankfully, they pay respectful attention to your words, with very few interruptions.

When students are answering a question or making a point, however, it is a different story altogether. After a few seconds of student talk, several classmates seize the opportunity to let their attention drift and to lapse into private chats. As a consequence, interesting contributions are ignored or drowned out, leaving the student who is meant to be the one doing the talking looking fed up.

How should you deal with this rudeness?

DOI: 10.4324/9781003440826-51

Avoid saying

"[Students' names], be quiet and listen when others are speaking."

Reframe for success

"Sorry, [name of student talking], can you pause for a moment, please. Someone has forgotten my expectations: when somebody else is talking, everybody listens."

Why does this work?

Drawing attention to the students who are interrupting can divide the class into two camps: those that try hard and answer questions and those who switch off when the first camp is talking. This can create an unintentional "swots" versus "rebels" split.

Alternatively, referring to classroom expectations in general terms illustrates that students are unified in the same respectful aim: showing good manners by paying attention to classmates. Pausing the student speaking – and then getting them to start again from the beginning after the reminder – demonstrates that each part of their valued contribution will always be heard.

Next steps

1. **Expect full attention for speakers –** Talking over students is clearly unacceptable. Yet other signs of poor attention when peers are speaking, such as turning around or looking out of the window, should also be addressed.
2. **Model politeness to the interrupted student –** Apologise for having to interrupt the speaking student and then thank them for waiting while you address the class. Displaying this level of politeness prompts others to eventually follow suit.
3. **Build on students' contributions –** To encourage full attention, ensure you bounce students' ideas on to others. What can they add to their classmate's comments? Do they agree with their answer? Students are more likely to listen if they can expect to have to respond to the initial input.

The students who hate sitting next to each other (#50)

The scenario

After what seemed like hours of tweaking and crossing out, you've arrived at a final seating plan. Every variable has been considered: behaviour points, prior attainment, quality of eyesight, students with the same first name … It's been a long, arduous process but the masterplan is now ready to be unveiled.

As students troop into the classroom, you allocate their seats with efficient briskness. Gradually, the desks fill. Everything is going well. But then you announce a pair of students who will share a desk. They both groan and share a look of disdain bordering on contempt. From that point on, they use any opportunity to complain about sitting next to each other.

How should you manage this unforeseen seating plan malfunction?

DOI: 10.4324/9781003440826-52

Avoid saying

"You're just going to have to learn to put up with one another."

Reframe for success

"I'll look again at my seating plan but where you sit will be my choice."

Why does this work?

Seating plans are an essential behaviour management tool. Allowing students to choose their seat rarely ends well. But by rigidly refusing to accept that these two students sitting next to each other is causing more problems than it solves, the teacher is stubbornly condemning themselves to ongoing unnecessary hassle.

A more flexible teacher will retain decision-making authority, yet be willing to consider reasonable changes. To avoid ancient grudges breaking to new classroom mutiny, it's better to swiftly amend plans. Students won't get to pick a preferred seat but they will get to be moved away when there is obvious mutual enmity.

Next steps

1. **Discuss seating issues discreetly** – Publicly asking students why they won't sit near each other can create an awkward scene. They may, for example, be ex-romantic partners who have just broken up. If you really need to know, ask in private.
2. **Review seating arrangements from time to time** – Occasionally reflect on the effectiveness of your seating plan. And if a refresh doesn't work, you can always revert to the first plan.
3. **Be wary of rigid arrangements** – Alphabetical order by surname? Boy/girl split on every table? These might seem like a quick and easy answer to seating plan creation, but they can be deeply problematic, especially if the same plan is used by all teachers in the school.

The student who is a prolific doodler (#51)

The scenario

Profound yet mundane, the artist's oeuvre challenges the viewer's cultural preconceptions. Each artwork imaginatively thrusts the onlooker into an aesthetic puzzle. Through the juxtaposition of the banal and the arresting, they interrogate ideas of chaos and conformity.

What appear to be primitive stickmen are, in reality, deeply meaningful comments on the human condition. Crude caricatures of friends and teachers provoke turbulently existential questions, like what is the purpose of art? Other questions include: why have I got the voice of a gallery curator in my head? Why does this student keep doodling during my lessons?

And, most importantly: should I put a stop to these artistic expressions?

DOI: 10.4324/9781003440826-53

Avoid saying	Reframe for success
"Your exercise book is not a sketchpad!"	"I don't mind seeing doodles on spare paper, as long as I'm also seeing your best work."

Why does this work?

Doodling is largely seen by teachers as a visual form of daydreaming. Frequent drawings in the margins of student work are usually interpreted as a sign of laziness or distraction. In some cases, they can be. But in many cases, doodling is an attempt to maintain attention, to avoid the brain switching off. Often, doodlers have just as much awareness of what is going on in class as the student who tracks the teacher throughout the lesson with devoted eyes.

If a student is doodling *and* producing work of a high standard, then there's little point making an issue out of it. Give them a spare sheet of paper so the presentation of their work isn't impaired and let them get on with it. If, however, elaborate doodles are symptomatic of an aversion to hard work, then tackle their lack of effort with the normal consequences.

Next steps

1. **Encourage them to set limits –** The cognitive benefits of doodling can evaporate over time. For this reason, help them avoid spending extended periods drawing, as their focus is likely to drift away from work eventually.
2. **Don't let them draw on tests –** Doodling may stimulate productivity, but seeing squiggles and cartoon images all over an assessment paper creates a poor impression. Discourage this strongly, as it could bring a cost in future.
3. **Discuss the impact of different types of doodling –** Research tells us that creating detailed sketches ultimately impedes students' concentration during complex learning. Encourage students, therefore, instead to stick to the filling in of simple shapes when doodling and only to do this for a brief period of time.

The class that is hard work for the last period of the day (#52)

The scenario

In the morning, they're angelic. Faces like celestial cherubs radiate innocence and attentiveness. The classroom is full of pleasant demeanours, quiet voices and scholarly efforts. Even the euphemistically "lively" students are compliant. No doubt their hushed behaviour can be explained by tiredness rather than natural studiousness, but you'll take it.

Afternoons are a different matter entirely. Gone are the saintly characteristics, replaced now by mischievous glances, bellowing voices and an aversion to hard graft. Those dormant students are making up for lost time, having shaken off their morning slumber in time for some afternoon hi jinx. Classroom visitors could be mistaken for thinking they've entered Dante's seventh circle. It's loud.

How can you manage these manic final periods of the day?

DOI: 10.4324/9781003440826-54

Avoid saying

"If you do some quiet work for fifteen minutes, I'll let you do something fun."

Reframe for success

"My expectations don't change throughout the day. Whispering voices only or we'll be working in silence."

Why does this work?

Faced with circumstances like these, it is understandable when teachers resort to the one of the oldest motivators in human history: bribery. Promising a more enticing activity than hard work works well in the short-term. Given the opportunity to avoid doing proper work, even the rowdiest of classes can stay quiet for a brief period.

Eventually, though, as the initial sugar rush of the bribe wears off, students will grow complacent and will start to mess around during the fun activity. Worst still is the long-term impact of tacitly admitting to a class that you can't control them in an afternoon. And therefore, the post-lunch period is for fun activities only, rather than serious study. Can you afford to write-off that amount of curriculum time?

Next steps

1. **Use a do now task to set expectations –** With a class like this, get into the routine of using a silent retrieval starter. The instructions on the board should be clear, as should the expectations about completing it individually in silence.
2. **Give precise volume instructions –** Vague instructions about acceptable noise levels (see #24) can lead to uncertainty and a creeping increase in volume. Be specific about noise parameters when you set the task.
3. **Employ general reminders –** A quick pep-talk can help students see the bigger picture: "We're nearing the end of the day and you've done well so far this period. It would be a real shame if I had to start giving out warnings at this stage."

The class that's unsettled while a student is thinking (#53)

The scenario

As questions go, it was a reasonably difficult one. But, nonetheless, you were expecting the student you asked to be able to answer it. After a few seconds they haven't said anything. Not "I don't know" or "can you repeat the question?". After 10 seconds the silence is starting to become slightly uncomfortable. Did they hear you say their name? Why aren't they answering you?

Seconds continue to ebb away painfully. Students begin to look at the silent student and exchange quizzical glances at each other. There are a few muffled sniggers and whispered comments. After 20, 25 seconds a palpable awkwardness hangs in the air. The class becomes increasingly restless and you're dying inside.

What should you do next?

DOI: 10.4324/9781003440826-55

Avoid saying

"Ok, if you don't know the answer we'll just move on."

Reframe for success

"I'm really pleased when students think about a tricky question. Let's show respect by giving everyone the time to think carefully."

Why does this work?

Teachers tend to expect students to answer questions after a surprisingly short period of time. Often, teachers push students for an answer, or rush in to "save" them, after just a few seconds of waiting. Because of our expertise, we tend to assume questions are more straightforward than they are.

Classes need to be taught to recognise the importance of careful reflection before answering. We need to model patience and not appear flustered when a student takes an age to respond to our questioning. Students need encouragement and training to avoid becoming distracted when other students are deep in thought.

Next steps

1. **Extend wait time for all questions –** By giving students longer wait times than we usually might, we advertise the fact that silent thinking is a normal part of our lessons. When we jump in constantly, we promote impatience among students.

2. **Allow whole class thinking time for complex questions –** Say you're giving the class 30 seconds to think because you'll be asking some students to answer this tricky question shortly. This helps them acclimatise to silence during longer wait times.

3. **Celebrate deep thinking –** Show that you're impressed when a student takes a long time before giving a thoughtful and considered response. This normalises longer wait times and the accompanying silence.

The class that doesn't mind negative phone calls home (#54)

The scenario

The behaviour of some of the class is intolerable. Yet again, you find yourself clutching a lengthy list of phone numbers. Once more, at the end of a tiring and dispiriting day, it's time to inform certain parents what their child has been up to during your lessons. For the best part of an hour you dial, explain, discuss and then hang up.

A few parents and guardians are supportive and promise to speak to their child as soon as they step through the door. Others are struggling themselves and aren't sure whether speaking to their child will make much difference. Some parents are defensive and seem to imply that you must have done something wrong to provoke the poor behaviour. Deflatingly, the next day you see little improvement from any of the students who received calls home.

How can you use parental contact to help modify their behaviour?

DOI: 10.4324/9781003440826-56

Avoid saying	Reframe for success
"That's enough! I'm phoning some of your parents again."	"I'm looking forward to speaking to the parents of those of you who have impressed me today."

Why does this work?

While negative calls to parents are sometimes essential, they tend to be an ineffective tool for students who cause repeated disruption in lessons. The first call might well prompt a change of behaviour after a sharp word from their parents, but over time this approach tends to lose its impact. Parents can become worn down by constant negative calls; students can become less motivated by what they see at their guardian's nagging.

On the other hand, positive phone calls can have a lasting effect on relationships. Let the class know that you're looking to call home with praise for two or three students each day and, over time, you hope to be able to find a reason to get around everyone in the class. The urge to impress their parents can be a strong motivator for most students.

Next steps

1. **Ensure positive calls are earned –** "Catch them doing something good" is sound advice but don't make calls home for students who simply don't deserve them. Premature rewards can cause complacency and lead to behaviour deteriorating.
2. **Follow positive calls with negatives where necessary –** Making an initial positive call home means that any subsequent negative calls are more likely to be acted upon. It's easier to work as a team when they already know you value their child.
3. **Schedule time to make calls –** Finding the time to make positive calls might seem like a drain but the sense of satisfaction from speaking to pleased parents can be huge. Friday afternoon calls in particular help end the week with a warm glow.

The student who keeps looking out of the window (#55)

The scenario

It's the start of summer. The sky resembles a child's painting: electric blue brush-strokes smeared across a cloudless horizon. A languid sun radiates a heat that is perfect for leisure but not ideal for those attempting work. Outside the classroom window, a lawnmower allows itself to be pushed around by a vest-wearing groundskeeper. It's a bucolic scene.

Most students, however, remain diligent despite the increasing temperature and the picturesque landscape. They're focused, with their eyes on their work. One student is different, of course. All year round, come rain, sleet, hail, shine or nondescript grey, they can be found gazing outside, attention anywhere other than inside your room.

How can you bring them from the outside world back to their books?

DOI: 10.4324/9781003440826-57

Avoid saying

"Stop looking out the window and get back on with your work."

Reframe for success

"I know our minds can wander when we're working but I don't want to see students staring out of the window."

Why does this work?

Attention is a fickle beast. Adults often find their thoughts drifting during meetings, presentations or writing reports. It may even happen while you're reading a stimulating book on behaviour management! So rather than giving immediate punishments to students taking in the view, offer an acknowledgement that this can happen naturally.

Yet we must also reinforce how frequent focus lapses are the enemy of learning. And that avoiding work by regularly gawping out of the window is not acceptable behaviour. A gentle reminder of expectations can help reset a student's concentration whereas a more confrontational rebuke can lead to further acts of defiant inattention.

Next steps

1. **Adjust your seating plan –** It may be worth tweaking your seating plan to ensure that window rubberneckers are located centrally in the room. While this might not completely cut off their exterior access, it should lessen the appeal of the outdoor scenes.

2. **Close the nearest blind –** If seating moves don't help, closing nearby blinds or curtains might well make a difference. Looking at a blank covering is far less appealing than an entertaining vista resplendent with nature and human activity.

3. **Change the room layout –** The nuclear option (best employed in a class where multiple students are window gazers) is a complete rearrangement of the room. It may be possible to ensure most students have the windows behind them in some rooms. Using rows to ensure all students are facing you may make a big difference.

The class that makes subtle racist "jokes" (#56)

The scenario

It's hard to describe what's happening. It's difficult to encapsulate but something untoward is taking place. It's subtle yet hard to miss. It's jokey yet very serious. The fact is that some students in the class have started calling another student "Shrek". Everyone laughs, including the student. But the deeper pain on their face can't be disguised by smiles and laughter.

In referencing the famously ugly cartoon ogre, they're implying the student shares those unattractive features. But there's something else going on here: Shrek has a different skin colour to the other characters in the film. This student has a different skin colour to everyone else in the class. Something tells you that this juvenile humour carries a racist subtext, an unspoken understanding that the student is being "othered."

What can you do to address this situation?

DOI: 10.4324/9781003440826-58

Avoid saying	Reframe for success
"That's racist and it's making [student's name] feel very uncomfortable."	"We're not calling each other names in this class. I will be speaking to some of you about this later."

Why does this work?

In situations where racism isn't obvious, calling it out directly can lead to things spiralling out of control. Publicly accusing students of racist behaviour in a context where the language isn't explicitly racist can trigger unintended repercussions. What's more, the student on the receiving end is unlikely to thank you for naming them and addressing it in front of the rest of the class. Their fake laughter demonstrates that discretion is needed.

To protect the vulnerable student, an immediate priority is to prohibit name calling, with sanctions for any student that continues to use them. After the lesson, detailed investigation is required. Speaking to students individually, including the student affected, will emphasise why the behaviour is unacceptable and why it can't be allowed to continue.

Next steps

1. **Liaise with pastoral leads** – It's likely that the "jokey" racism is happening elsewhere in the school. Speak to pastoral leads to ensure that the student is fully supported, and the school takes a wider approach to tackling the issue.
2. **Look out for other signs of prejudice** – Subtle verbal abuse may be just one way that the student is being targeted. Keep a close eye out for other unacceptable behaviours that peers may use to ostracise and bully the student.
3. **Ensure the curriculum is inclusive** – It's hard to educate students about the importance of diversity if the curriculum itself is unrepresentative. Make sure your resources and language are inclusive.

The class that ridicules students for working hard (#57)

The scenario

For the majority of the students in your class, learning is seen as something that is forced upon them. Work is viewed as a means to an end, to be done only under duress. Tasks will be completed begrudgingly, with the minimal amount of effort exerted. Given the choice, they'd rather be anywhere else than in a classroom, being educated against their will.

A handful of students see things differently. They are keen to excel, enthusiastic about gaining knowledge and keen to gain your approval. These students thrive when given challenging work and respond well to your critical feedback. As a result of their scholarly dedication, these students are, of course, mocked by their more lethargic peers.

How can you stop these students being labelled as swots, geeks and nerds?

DOI: 10.4324/9781003440826-59

Avoid saying

"I wish all of you worked as hard as [students' names]."

Reframe for success

"I expect everyone to work hard in my class. We will celebrate each other's achievements, not put them down."

Why does this work?

Placing diligent students up on a pedestal as a role model for others to emulate may seem like a sensible approach. But in all likelihood, it will backfire, leaving them even more exposed to ridicule by their peers. Being thrust into the glare of peer scrutiny will probably heighten their embarrassment and encourage other students to target them further.

A more effective approach is a general reinforcement of expectations about effort and productivity. Alongside this, students should hear constant reminders about appropriate ways to respond to each other. Changing the culture of a class takes time. But, eventually, teasing will decline, and unmotivated students will reflect more on their own work ethic.

Next steps

1. **Don't have obvious favourites** – While some students are more enjoyable to teach than others, we must avoid displays of favouritism. By constantly cheerleading for certain students, we undermine our neutrality and expose them to further scorn.

2. **Be careful about oversharing their efforts** – If we make constant use of the same students' work as examples of excellence, other students will become demoralised and feel that there is no point working hard, as their work will never be showcased.

3. **Make cold call your default questioning style** – Students are often called swots for raising their hands to answer questions. By adopting cold call as your standard questioning style, you can remove that possibility. Ensuring that all students answer questions regularly removes the voluntary element.

The student who only works when you're stood over them (#58)

The scenario

Like workers caught napping by a feared manager, this student leaps into action as soon as you turn up. Look busy: the boss is here! Before your arrival, they stare into nothingness, thoughts far removed from the task that sits before them. They know how to play this game. As long as they're doing something while you stand and monitor them, they feel immune to a reprimand about their lack of effort.

The moment you leave, however, they down tools with remarkable abruptness. Thumbs up from the lookout. The pressure is off. It's time for a well-earned breather. So, you head back to their desk and, sure enough, the game recommences. They begin where they left off, displaying a convincing performance of studiousness for the period that you're present. Then you trudge off and...

What's the best strategy to keep them on task throughout?

DOI: 10.4324/9781003440826-60

Avoid saying

"You need to stay focused on your work."

Reframe for success

"I'll be back in five minutes. By that time, I expect you to have achieved the following..."

Why does this work?

Some students see work as a game of cat and mouse, only to be undertaken when you're in the vicinity. Reminders to these students to stay on task, and exhortations to work harder, are unlikely to make much of a difference. They are currently expending effort for one reason only: to keep you off their back temporarily. Pep talks are unlikely to cut it.

With students who choose when to turn on the tap of productivity, more direct methods are required. You're not playing their game any longer. Instead of vague jollying along, you will need to be clear about the exact progress you expect them to make in the precise timescale you give them. There's a far greater likelihood of this moving them on when you depart.

Next steps

1. **Use the dot or put them on the clock** – Place a dot in the margin to give a visual indication of expected completion. If you really want to emphasise your point, adding a time deadline will further amplify the sense of urgency.
2. **Allude to non-specific sanctions** – Being vague about sanctions motivates most students to speed up. "If you don't get this done in the allocated time, we're going to have a problem" conjures up a range of potential unappealing consequences.
3. **Take poor productivity very seriously** – Some students may continue to produce little work despite strict parameters. In this case, a sustained rejection of work must be seen as an act of defiance and should be sanctioned in the same way as other refusals to follow instructions.

The student who falls asleep in lessons (#59)

The scenario

Right then, children. Are you sitting comfortably? Then I shall begin. There was once a very busy teacher who put a lot of time into preparing interesting and informative lessons. One day, however, when they were delivering this fastidiously organised material, they came upon a student who was paying no attention to the fascinating facts being bestowed upon them.

Indeed, this troublesome student appeared to have been touched by the soporific finger of Hypnos. All of a sudden, the signs of sleep became quickly evident: fallen eyelids, nodding head and a faint trickle of drool from the corner of the mouth. The student had left the land of the conscious.

What should the unfortunate teacher do about this sleepy student?

DOI: 10.4324/9781003440826-61

Avoid saying	Reframe for success
"How dare you fall asleep in my class?"	"We need to have a chat about your constant tiredness in my lesson."

Why does this work?

Teachers are miracle workers. But unless you have the ability to teach via hypnosis, you will be unable to impart any knowledge to a sleeping student. Getting annoyed by students dropping off into dreamland is understandable. Yet waking a student with an angry admonishment is likely to lead to an irritable backlash.

Instead, a calm discussion after the event – then informing parents and pastoral leads – is a more sensible way forward. State the facts dispassionately: there is nothing you can do as a teacher to help their child make progress if they are so tired that they are falling asleep during class. Unless there is a medical or safeguarding issue, the parents will need to put clear boundaries in place to enable you to help their child achieve academically.

Next steps

1. **Resist the urge to wake them up suddenly** – Dropping a hefty book on the desk of a snoring student may seem tempting. But it could provide a nasty shock and leave them feeling humiliated. A more professional gentle word in their ear should suffice.
2. **Look out for patterns across the week** – Are their snooze sessions more frequent on Monday mornings after late nights at the weekend? Or do they flag later in the week. Noticing these trends can help identify issues during parental discussions.
3. **Ensure they catch up** – You might not be able to get much useful out of them when they're lethargic but insist on them catching up on the work they missed while dozing. This will provide an incentive for them to arrive at class more refreshed in future.

The class that takes ages to find the relevant section (#60)

The scenario

You're ready to begin. You provide a very simple instruction: the page number to which they need to turn; the relevant section they need to find; the question number at which they need to begin. It's extremely straightforward. Basic stuff. Surveying the room, you see eager eyes waiting for you to begin.

This simple instruction, however, is seemingly too difficult to be followed by several members of your class. "What was that page number again?," "What are we meant to be doing?," "What question did you say we're starting at?" It's enough to drive anyone mad. Indeed, the rest of the class find it just as frustrating as you.

How can you ensure they listen to your instructions first time?

DOI: 10.4324/9781003440826-62

Avoid saying	Reframe for success
"Turn to page 74… I've just told you that. Turn to *page 74*!"	"Listen carefully while I tell you where we're starting from. Turn to page 74."

Why does this work?

When we front load instructions with a cue that important information is about to be given, students are more likely to pay close attention to that information. It signals to students that we're going to give vital instructions that are both time sensitive and integral to their understanding of the task that follows.

In this context, repeating instructions is a mistake because it maintains inattentive students' dependency on you. As students realise that you're not prepared to give simple instructions more than once, they will be forced to pay more attention to your initial words. By restating instructions again, you're enabling their lack of focus. But by ignoring their requests and simply continuing you're making it clear that if they don't pay heed to what you say first time round it is their problem to solve, not yours.

Next steps

1. **Make the relevant section visible –** As a visual prompt, note the starting point on the board or place the relevant section under a visualiser. Instead of reiterating the information, point to the prompt in silence.
2. **Allow other students to silently help –** Give a glance to the student sitting next to them, nod towards the student who is stuck, and get them to pass on the relevant information discreetly.
3. **Circulate while reading –** If a student still doesn't know what they should be doing, move around the class as you read aloud or are giving further instructions. Silently point to the part they should be focussing on.

The student who avoids challenging work (#61)

The scenario

To try and meet the needs of all students, you differentiate your resources. Straightforward Bronze tasks can be done independently by nearly all students. Silver tasks are trickier, with some students requiring assistance. Gold tasks are challenging. These are given out to just a few students, but others can progress on to these worksheets if they finish the silver tasks.

There are certain students you feel are capable of having a crack at Gold work. One student in particular has the potential to excel at most subjects. But they are very reluctant to push themselves. They like to relax in the steady waters of the Bronze questions, then tentatively dip into the Silver questions. Rarely do they immerse themselves in complex Gold depths.

What can you do to get them swimming in more challenging waters?

DOI: 10.4324/9781003440826-63

Avoid saying

"I'd like to see you try doing some of the extension activities."

Reframe for success

"I'm starting you off with this trickier work. I'll give you some help if you get stuck."

Why does this work?

Differentiated activities and extension tasks provide students with an opt-out. A small minority of students will take this opt-out because it requires less energy than taking on extra work. Many more, however, will take the opt-out as a result of peer pressure. After all, who wants to be seen asking for extra work of the difficult variety when you can pretend you didn't have the time to get around to doing the complicated stuff?

When students are given challenging work from the outset, however, they tend to persevere, ignorant of the undemanding work they might otherwise have been given. Instead of coasting through a less taxing activity, they grapple with the complexities that lay before them. Indeed, they grow to enjoy the challenge. Over time, complex work becomes the main course of learning rather than a side dish for those who have already finished.

Next steps

1. **Explain why they're getting harder work** – Rather than just doling out the worksheets, let reticent students know that you're giving them more difficult work because you have high expectations of them and, with effort, they'll meet them.

2. **Rethink your use of extension and differentiation** – If harder tasks are routinely swerved by coasting students, remove them as an option altogether. Build in challenge as the norm, so that all students are expected to attempt these tasks.

3. **Offer live feedback to maintain effort levels** – Timely feedback is a vital factor in motivating students. When complex tasks are being undertaken, effective feedback in the moment is even more important. Giving specific areas for improvement during lessons helps them to taste success and maintain their effort levels.

The student who won't leave the room when asked (#62)

The scenario

You've had enough. For the duration of the lesson so far their behaviour has been poor. You've reminded them of your expectations. When that made no difference, you moved to the next stage of the behaviour policy. And yet they've continued to disrupt the class.

So you've asked them to get their work and leave the room. You've informed them where they need to go. But they haven't moved at all. Fixed to their seat, with arms crossed over their chest, they aren't budging. They heard you all right, but in one last dramatic act of defiance, they aren't shifting.

What should your next move be?

DOI: 10.4324/9781003440826-64

Avoid saying

"I've told you to get out. Now move!"

Reframe for success

"I'm going to give you a couple of minutes to make the right decision. Let's not turn this into a bigger thing than it needs to be."

Why does this work?

Students refuse to leave the room for a variety of reasons. First, they feel they're the victim of some kind of injustice, that they don't deserve this punishment. Second, they're shocked that you've instigated the ultimate classroom sanction and are almost numbed into inertia. Third, they're fearful of the consequences of being sent out and hope that if they stay long enough you'll relent and let them stay.

Regardless of their reason for refusing to move, the simple fact is that they have to go. The question now is how best to extricate them with minimum disruption for the rest of the class. For this reason, a public stand-off will only make things worse. Instead, get the class working then have a whispered word to the student. Allowing them the opportunity to back down without an audience can help avoid humiliation and encourage them to move.

Next steps

1. **Don't stand over them –** While they consider their next move, leave their area of the classroom. Return to your desk or support students elsewhere in the class. Giving them space increases the chance that they will depart through their own volition.

2. **Stay calm when help arrives –** If you have to call a senior colleague for support in removing them, avoid ranting about how bad they've been. If possible, step aside and let your colleague deal with the situation. Let off any steam in a follow-up chat.

3. **Have the same standards near the end of the lesson –** Teachers occasionally let students off if the lesson is nearing a close. When this happens, students can take advantage. If they need to go, they need to go. Enlist SLT support if you don't have time to deal with the aftermath.

The class that asks for a fun end-of-term lesson (#63)

The scenario

Exhausted, the pack nears the end of their mammoth journey. Fatigued by months of drudgery, the bedraggled cubs are desperate for a break. Close to the sanctuary of home, they can smell the possibility of rest and relaxation. Physically and mentally spent, they search for a sign that they will soon be able to pause. At last, they reach their destination.

An epic journey with their elders has taught the creatures so much; it has also left them overwhelmed. They yearn for less taxing activities, requiring little effort from brain or body. Gingerly, one of the pluckier cubs approaches the group's alpha: "Excuse me. Please can we have a fun lesson today?"

Should you give in to a request to abandon learning?

DOI: 10.4324/9781003440826-65

Avoid saying

"Yes, you can watch a movie. Let's have a vote on which film to see."

Reframe for success

EITHER "No, that's not possible. We've got too much work to do." *OR* "Ok, as a treat we'll be doing this today..."

Why does this work?

Certain schools have strict policies about teaching proper lessons right up until the end of term. If you work in one of these schools, it's your professional duty to uphold this policy. Going maverick risks landing you in trouble with your line manager. It also, of course, undermines colleagues who stick to the rules. But if your school doesn't have a policy then the choice is yours.

Some teachers will tell you that learning time is precious, so end of term movies, quizzes or parties are not to be tolerated. Others will argue that students deserve a breather after a term of toil, and one lesson of fun isn't going to hurt them. If you subscribe to the latter view, avoid allowing students to vote. You'll end up with a split decision and will spend the rest of the lesson dealing with students who are grumpy about not getting their preferred activity.

Next steps

1. **Explain your decision –** Whatever your take on "free" lessons, explain your stance. It helps students to see that it's not an arbitrary decision when it's based on factors like amount of curriculum time or whether they've worked well during the term.

2. **Consider linking fun to learning –** A third option is to allow a relaxed activity that nonetheless boosts their knowledge. A movie version of a text they've studied or a quiz related to a recent topic offers a welcome compromise for conflicted teachers.

3. **Think about seating plans –** Students often associate fun lessons with a relaxation of seating plans. Are you prepared for the increased noise and potential silliness that can come with this? Outline your precise expectations before the fun begins.

The class that uses homophobic language (#64)

The scenario

Everything is gay, apparently. This cheap calculator is gay. Those trainers are gay. A student's drawing is gay. The school's next residential trip is gay. This topic is definitely gay. In this class, the adjective "gay" doesn't just mean homosexual. It is now used as a catch-all insult, a synonym for "rubbish," "stupid" and "unappealing."

During lessons you often hear students using the alternative meaning of this well-known adjective. They're not being directly homophobic to each other. They're not calling their peers gay or making explicit statements that express openly derogatory views about homosexuality. But you know very well that using this word in this way is not acceptable.

How can you stop the use of this homophobic language?

DOI: 10.4324/9781003440826-66

Avoid saying	Reframe for success
"Stop being mean to each other."	"Do you understand what the word "gay" means? So why are you using it as an insult?"

Why does this work?

Characterising these insults as general meanness is inadequate. It is unlikely to shift students' attitudes to usage of the word. Referring to this behaviour as "mean" fails to take into account the wider cultural context of language use. Students need to be reminded of the weight of their words; labelling this behaviour as merely unkind doesn't achieve this.

By focusing on the usual meaning of "gay" (homosexual), students are forced to recognise the prejudice revealed when they use it pejoratively. They need to know that when they use "gay" to describe something as substandard or unwanted, they're effectively saying people who are homosexual are embarrassing or inferior to heterosexuals. Faced with this obvious discrimination, students are unlikely to carry on using the adjective in a throwaway manner.

Next steps

1. **Take firm action against future usage** – Once students are aware of the full implications of using "gay" as a slur, you will need to treat any further uses as a deliberate, provocative homophobic act, to be dealt with by senior colleagues.
2. **Develop their vocabulary** – If students wish to display harmless disparagement about something, equip them with an impressive vocabulary to do so. Think "unappealing" or "vacuous" rather than "dumb."
3. **Use inclusive language in your classroom** – Do your resources and lesson materials use examples that are exclusively about relationships between men and women? Heteronormative language can cement non-inclusive mindsets among your students.

The class that doesn't do homework (#65)

The scenario

It's an essential component of academic success. Whether it's reading a book, completing a page of sums or revising for an upcoming assessment, homework makes a significant difference to student outcomes. In lessons, the class does their best and works hard for you. Completing work outside of school is, however, a wholly different situation.

Whenever it's time to collect in the allocated homework, all you generally receive is a litany of excuses. Any work that is submitted is usually rushed or copied verbatim from a webpage. Detentions and phone calls home make little difference.

How can you get them to complete homework?

DOI: 10.4324/9781003440826-67

Avoid saying

"Hands up everyone who hasn't done homework. Right, you're on my detention list again."

Reframe for success

"I'll be coming round soon to collect homework. I'm looking forward to seeing work that's really going to help you improve in this subject."

Why does this work?

In the short term, detentions and other sanctions might boost homework uptake. But to build and sustain a culture of homework completion, you need to work on students' intrinsic motivation. In other words, you need to convince students that homework is not just a chore to be done to avoid getting in trouble or something to be done so they get a reward, like a nice shiny gold star.

Instead, you need to help them to realise that homework is something that students finish because it is valuable in its own right. They need to see that, in the long run, doing homework can be inherently satisfying, as it enhances their knowledge and leads to them feeling more confident about their progress in the subject.

Next steps

1. **Don't set homework for the sake of it –** Tell students you won't be giving them homework just because the timetable demands it. Let them know that every piece of work you set will be vital to their progress. And stick to this approach!
2. **Show how homework completion boosts progress –** To reinforce this message, make explicit links between success with tasks in class and work that's been done at home. This will motivate them to complete further homework.
3. **Take away the social rewards for non-completion –** If some students consistently fail to hand things in and enjoy the peer group kudos this brings, take away the audience. Collect homework discreetly and don't advertise who is on the detention list!

The student who says the topic is boring (#66)

The scenario

As explanations go, this is one of your finest. Taking the intimidating weight of information on this notoriously complex topic, you're offering a well-sequenced and accessible summary of the key ideas. The subject matter may seem drier than dustbowl tumbleweed, but you're providing a textbook example of how to break down challenging information.

In a state of flow, you're just about to reach an emphatic conclusion. These final words will tie together and illuminate the significant strands of thought on this difficult topic. And, as you near the climax, a student interjects… Loudly and rudely, they rock their head back to the ceiling, throw up their arms and, for their classmates' benefit, say "This is so boring!".

Deeply irritated, how should you react?

DOI: 10.4324/9781003440826-68

Avoid saying

"If you think this is boring, wait until we start learning about ...!"

Reframe for success

"It might seem dull at the moment but stick with it and I think you'll find things that interest you eventually."

Why does this work?

Working with young people requires vast reserves of patience. An abrupt and bad-mannered interruption of this nature saps these reserves. But not rising to this provocation is important. Threatening to deploy the subject's unappealing aspects to bore a cheeky student into submission will not improve their motivation, or that of their peers.

If a student continues to make strident comments, you'll need to deal with it as insolence. Yet a better initial approach is to respond earnestly to the complaint. Acknowledging why they might feel like that to begin with – and explaining that you'll try to inspire them to change their opinion over time – should result in them giving the topic a chance.

Next steps

1. **Try not to take it personally** – We might be tempted to see rude comments as a personal attack and retaliate with slights of our own. Saying "only boring people get bored" might temporarily relieve our annoyance but it won't help the situation.

2. **Don't apologise in advance** – Wary of teaching unexciting topics, teachers sometimes make pre-emptive apologies. But a statement like "sorry this topic isn't particularly interesting" is a guaranteed way to turn students off from the outset.

3. **Ensure students taste success** – Students being engaged is a welcome sign, but it's a poor proxy for learning. Focus instead on making sure that students have some initial success with a topic. Doing well on a test will boost motivation more than snazzy lessons that attempt to enliven a topic that might be deemed tedious.

The class that is noisy when you circulate the room (#67)

The scenario

The class is well-trained at staying quiet while you speak from the front. But whenever you start to circulate during individual seat work, it's another matter entirely. To begin with, as you go to help struggling students, there's a bit of mild chatter. It's possibly related to the work, so you let it slide.

But, while you focus on providing detailed support, the noise continues to rise. Quiet chat becomes a noticeable hubbub. A noticeable hubbub becomes an increasing racket. An increasing racket becomes a full-blown uproar, an environment where purposeful thought and communication can no longer occur.

How can you prevent this happening the moment you start to work the room?

 DOI: 10.4324/9781003440826-69

Avoid saying

"Shhhh! I can't think straight with this noise."

Reframe for success

"With this amount of background noise, I'm not able to help any of you. Whispering voices only, or we go to full silence."

Why does this work?

Of all the behaviour management techniques that teachers deploy, shushing students has to be one of the most ineffective. Initially, shushing – like its close relative, the imperative "Be quiet!" – gains momentary respite. The class falls silent for a brief time, before the din is re-established. After a while, the shush joins the background noise, destined to be ignored.

The alternative response explains why the background noise is a problem and provides a precise acceptable volume level. The ultimatum must be stuck to: if general chatter continues, then silence must be maintained. This sets a clear boundary for students. Some work-related discussion is fine but only if it doesn't impede the concentration of others.

Next steps

1. **Lower your voice when giving support –** To promote the need for a quiet classroom in this context, ensure that your voice is also modified. By whispering, or giving silent written feedback, you're modelling the importance of quietness to aid concentration.

2. **Position yourself to check for talkers –** A chatting outbreak is more likely to happen when you have your back to the majority of the class. Before you arch over the desk, position yourself so you can keep an eye on as much of the room as possible.

3. **Stand at the back of the room –** Once you've insisted on silence, identifying which students are responsible for the continued noise is often easier from the back of the room. When students can't see your line of vision, they're more likely to be spotted.

The class that's deflated by poor assessment results (#68)

The scenario

After several hours marking the test papers, the results are in. They are not good. To say you're disappointed would be an understatement. All those hours of teaching. All that dedicated assessment preparation. All the effort of marking the papers. And the responses are riddled with errors, misconceptions and sloppy mistakes.

Inevitably, as you hand the papers back, heads drop. Confronted with the stark scores scribbled on their front sheet, faces turn crimson and mouths subside into frowns. Tears trickle down some students' cheeks. Others sit and stare at the desk, stunned and frustrated by their woeful performance.

What can you say to pull them out of this motivational abyss?

DOI: 10.4324/9781003440826-70

Avoid saying

"These results aren't good enough. You're all going to fail unless you improve dramatically."

Reframe for success

"I know you're disappointed. But if you act on my feedback, you'll see a big improvement next time."

Why does this work?

Most school assessments don't really matter that much! That might sound controversial but unless the assessment dictates whether students get into a certain school or university, or can follow a particular career, they aren't the be-all and end-all. We would, of course, prefer our students to flourish in all tests and mock exams. Nonetheless, we need them to see that, as long as they've done their best, these run-throughs are not ultimately decisive.

By bolstering the class – even if we're worried about their current performance – we convey the message that practice assessments are places where mistakes are expected. From these instructive mistakes, we can highlight areas to work on and unearth crucial knowledge gaps to be solved by more effective revision strategies. Berating them will deflate them further. Ultimately, reassurance – accompanied by diagnostic feedback – will be more motivational.

Next steps

1. **Take responsibility for your own shortcomings** – After disastrous results, be self-reflective and honest with the class. Point out areas that you should have covered in more detail and take ownership of things you perhaps didn't explain well.

2. **Reinforce the habits of excellence** – Use this failure as an opportunity to remind them about the importance of showing resilience and acting upon robust critique.

3. **Give them an opportunity to be successful** – Once you've allowed students to digest what went wrong, and have modelled what they should have done, give them a chance to sit a similar, but low-stakes, test so that they can experience success and quickly regain motivation.

The student who breaks wind or burps during a lesson (#69)

The scenario

Shortly after lunchtime, the class are getting on with their work. While they work their way through a silent extended activity, you sit at your desk and take the opportunity to catch up with some of your own work. In this peaceful environment both you and the class are getting plenty of work done.

From nowhere, there's an eruption of noise. It may be a discordant belch emitted from a student's mouth. Or, if you're more unlucky, it might be the rousing trumpet of a silence-puncturing fart. Either way, the class's attention has been shifted entirely from the work before them to the source of the voluminous emissions. Hilarity reigns.

What's the best way for you to deal with this most unwelcome interruption?

 DOI: 10.4324/9781003440826-71

Avoid saying

"That's disgusting. You should be ashamed of yourself!"

Reframe for success

"Accidental noises happen but if I think they're done on purpose I will not be impressed."

Why does this work?

Disruption of this kind can be placed into two categories. First, a student burps or breaks wind, turns scarlet faced with embarrassment, while the class laughs heartily at their misfortune. In this case, there is little point adding to their social awkwardness by making a big fuss about what's happened. Instead, ask the class to settle down and deal with any students who prolong the disruption.

The second type of student will, by contrast, burp or break wind with theatrical aplomb. Rather than feeling humiliated by the class's laughter they will smile and enjoy the attention brought about by their breach of good manners. In these circumstances, while we might assume that the noise was deliberate, it's hard to prove it in the first instance. A general reminder of expectations, therefore, with a subtle warning about repeat occurrences, is the best approach.

Next steps

1. **Sanction further instances –** Following a restating of expectations, treat further outbreaks of wind as deliberate disruption and sanction accordingly.
2. **Open windows as necessary –** While the laughter may quickly subside, noxious fumes may remain. Where possible, allow fresh air to circulate discreetly.
3. **Reinforce expectations about drinking –** Allowing students to have a sip of water during class is sensible practice in most instances (science labs being one notable exception). But if drinking leads to frequent burping, revisit your classroom rules.

The class that asks to listen to music while working (#70)

The scenario

You've explained the task carefully, modelled the success criteria and given them all the resources required to complete the work. All is calm; all is quiet. They are ready to begin.

Unexpectedly, a hand shoots up. Is it ok, they ask, for us to listen to music? They'll keep the volume down to a reasonable level, they promise. It's just a matter of slipping in their earphones and pressing play. Other teachers let them listen to music while working. What's more, they assure you, it really helps them concentrate. They definitely work better with their earphones in. There are nods of agreement from others, who also feel they would benefit from being allowed to listen to music while working.

What should you say to this request?

DOI: 10.4324/9781003440826-72

Avoid saying

"You can listen to music as long as it's quiet and you keep working."

Reframe for success

"I know you think music helps you focus but success in my class requires your full attention."

Why does this work?

The minute you permit one student's request to listen to music, you've effectively promoted it to the rest of the class as an acceptable study habit. Each time you set the class on any independent or extended activities, you'll be fielding frequent requests to stick their earphones in. Once Pandora's (beat)box has been opened, you won't be able to close the lid on the chaos of inattention it will unleash upon your lessons.

Instead, by sticking to your guns and insisting that your lesson will be a place where silent working is an expected part of most lessons, you'll be promoting close, undivided focus on work. Furthermore, you won't be undermining colleagues who don't want students listening to music in their lessons.

Next steps

1. **Show them the research** – There's a wealth of evidence to show that study is far less effective when accompanied by music. This is especially true of music with lyrical content. They might think it helps them learn but in reality it doesn't.

2. **Explain your decision** – Students often become frustrated when they aren't allowed to do things that they think help them concentrate. But by making clear that you're helping them learn more effectively they're more likely to accept your decision.

3. **Acclimatise them to silent working** – Where silent periods of work are seen as unusual, students are much more likely to try to fill that gap with other variants of noise. Make silent lesson sections the norm and they'll adjust to them.

The class that passes notes around (#71)

The scenario

Something odd is going on. You've not yet sussed out what it is but something untoward is happening. Your teacher Spidey senses are tingling. An electric current of suspicion is pulsing through your nerve endings. They're up to something. Muffled laughter. Furtive hand gestures. Movement that betrays a lack of focus on the work. But what is it?

Like a bird of prey scanning the horizon, you spot an almost imperceptibly small rectangle of paper moving across the classroom. The folded scrap is being shifted rapidly from hand to hand. Ah! They're passing notes. Sensing your opportunity, you pounce and confiscate the offending origami memo.

What should your next step be?

DOI: 10.4324/9781003440826-73

Avoid saying

"I can't believe what I've just read. What a nasty thing to pass around!"

Reframe for success

"We'll discuss this later. For now, let's get back on with our work."

Why does this work?

Discussing the contents of a note that's been shared around a classroom has the inevitable effect of derailing an already disrupted lesson. Further investigation will need to take place: What does it mean? Who wrote it? How many students read it, rather than just passing it along?

The best time to address these issues is at the end of the lesson, ideally with a small group of students who are likely ringleaders. Unless the contents of the note are offensive or a safeguarding issue, a sensible approach when sanctioning behaviour is to address the lesson disruption caused by note-passing, rather than the note's contents.

Next steps

1. **Think about whether you really want to know** – While some notes may contain innocent enough messages about students' romantic affections, others may involve a personal insult about you. While the note-taking behaviour needs to be tackled, you might decide that the note itself is better chucked straight into a bin unread.
2. **Ensure desks are free of clutter** – Spotting students doing things like passing notes can be trickier when your line of vision is obscured by things like bags or large pencil cases. Ensure students put these away as a matter of course.
3. **Follow-up on pastoral issues** – Notes will occasionally throw up a possible concern about a particular student. Even if it seems innocuous, it's always worth referring it to their pastoral lead.

The students who are demotivated by "low ability" grouping (#72)

The scenario

In a primary setting, they can be found sitting on an allocated table. We might give this table a cute name, such as the hedgehog or acorn table, or something more neutral, such as the blue or yellow table. But the students occupying these chairs will see through this rebranding. They'll still be demotivated by knowing they're the designated strugglers: kids who aren't as good at reading or subtracting or forming words in cursive handwriting.

In a secondary setting, they can be found in a separate group. We might assign these classes alphabetical codes, such as 8X or 10C, or something creative like 7BRONTE or 11SEACOLE. But the kids will soon see through our efforts to disguise their position in the intelligence hierarchy. They'll be demotivated by their classification as bottom set material.

DOI: 10.4324/9781003440826-74

Avoid saying

"You've been put in this group because you need extra help."

Reframe for success

"I'm going to help you realise that you're better at this than you might think you are."

How can you boost the confidence of these demoralised students?

Why does this work?

Although it might be accurate, the struggler label does great harm to our confidence. Like the uncoordinated child who's always last to be picked for a sports team, being placed in a "low ability" group can land a near fatal blow to our self-esteem. In these circumstances, the last thing students want to hear is a frank reminder of how they're viewed.

The slow process of rebuilding their self-efficacy begins with a statement that outlines some key messages. First, that you're dedicated to helping them get better at the things they find tricky. Second, that they shouldn't pay much attention to the inner voice that says they're rubbish compared to students in the other groups. Third, by ensuring that they taste some success in the topic, you're going to restore their academic confidence.

Next steps

1. **Stop using the word "weak"** – This adjective suggests that ability is fixed and that students are inherently good or bad at something. Instead, espouse the mantra that with practice and effective feedback everybody can get better at anything.
2. **Show they're getting challenging work** – Students who have fallen behind don't catch up through being given easy work. Make it clear from the outset that you will be giving them challenging work, as well as the support to be able to access it.
3. **Provide opportunities for movement** – If we accept that ability isn't fixed, then we need to create chances for students to move between ability groups when they earn it. In an ideal world, there would be greater mixing between groups. But if that's not possible, maintain motivation by allowing students to step up when ready.

The class that makes negative comments about colleagues (#73)

The scenario

If you were to list characteristics of a dream class, this group of students would tick almost all the boxes. Hard-working? Tick. Kind to one another? Tick. Intellectually curious? Tick. Respectful towards you? Tick. You can have a laugh with them. You can go off topic with them. You can even trust them for a couple of minutes while you nip to the photocopier.

But there's a problem. A single flaw that prevents them from nearing perfection. They keep slagging off your colleagues. Sometimes it comes in the form of minor gripes about support staff who are too strict during break times. At other times it emerges as a rude comment about another teacher, criticising several aspects of their personality. They've even asked for your opinion on this colleague, egging you on to join in the dissing.

How should you respond to these awkward comments?

DOI: 10.4324/9781003440826-75

Avoid saying	Reframe for success
"I know [colleague's name] can be grumpy but they're alright when you get to know them."	"I won't stand for any unkind comments about other adults."

Why does this work?

A sure-fire way of gaining popularity with a class is through a lukewarm endorsement of colleagues. This popularity, however, comes at a heavy cost. First, it seriously undermines the member of staff. Second, this unprofessionalism also encourages meanness among students. How can we ask them to be kind about each other if we can't manage to be kind about other adults?

Our thoughts about the colleague are utterly irrelevant. Whether the students might have a valid opinion is completely beside the point. If you do have any concerns about a colleague's approach to dealing with students, then take it up directly with them in a polite, non-confrontational manner. If need be, speak to your line manager. But never sell them short with students; it will come back to bite you. And you'll deserve that bite.

Next Steps

1. **Be careful about getting embroiled in disputes** – Students often look to favoured teachers to intervene on their behalf in disputes with less favoured teachers. Unless you were present, and can make a helpful intervention, avoid getting involved.
2. **Model courtesy** – It's a simple fact that not all adults get along. But in your public dealings with colleagues who you're not that keen on, it's vital that you model politeness and respect.
3. **Watch your body language** – Even if your tone is courteous, your body language might reveal your true feelings to perceptive students. Maintain a professional posture, especially after a disliked colleague has just left your room.

The student who keeps asking silly questions (#74)

The scenario

On the whole, they're a great class. The vast majority are enthusiastic about their learning and are keen to contribute to interesting discussions about a variety of topics. They respond well to your questioning and listen attentively during your explanations. The only time they get unsettled is when one student starts playing up.

Today's lesson follows a familiar pattern. All is ticking along well until this particular student sticks their hand in the hair, waiting patiently for you to call on them. You're hesitant, however; you've been caught out before. This student likes to ask daft questions, designed to elicit giggles from the rest of the class and disrupt the previously purposeful environment.

How should you respond to this raised hand?

DOI: 10.4324/9781003440826-76

Avoid saying

"What is it *now*? Go on then …"

Reframe for success

"Is this question sensible and relevant to the topic?"

Why does this work?

In this situation, just because a student has their hand raised it doesn't mean that they are entitled to be heard. If you suspect that they are going to sabotage your lesson with a verbal hand grenade, you have every right to check that their contribution isn't of a puerile nature. If they assure you that it will be sensible and it turns out to be silly, then that is deliberate and defiant disruption and needs to be dealt with accordingly.

Invariably, asking a student if it's going to be relevant deprives them of the opportunity to spring an unhelpful question or comment on you. Usually, they drop their hand in a deflated manner and retreat to a state of silence. Gradually, they'll learn that there is no place for silly questions in your classroom.

Next steps

1. **Enable them to contribute positively** – Where students seek attention in a negative way, find opportunities for them to contribute in a positive manner. Showcase their good work or ask them questions that you know they can answer well.

2. **Go over to them for a quiet discussion** – When their hand goes up during silent work, don't allow them to ask the question in front of the class. Go over and ask them to whisper the question to you instead, which reduces potential disruption.

3. **Pretend to take them seriously** – The student who poses immature questions is looking for an annoyed response from you to amuse their peers. Tackling these questions with mock earnestness can be effective at stopping this source of fun.

The class that questions the point of the subject (#75)

The scenario

There are things about the subjects we teach that we don't particularly enjoy. Certain topics might seem dull, unnecessary or irrelevant. Little wonder that students occasionally query the need to learn some stuff that the curriculum tells us we have to cover.

Questions like these will sometimes crop up. When am I ever going to use trigonometry in real life? Why do I need to know what material Roman soldiers' uniforms were made out of? How is a knowledge of iambic pentameter going to help me in my future career? Even with topics we love, it's not always easy to respond convincingly to these enquiries.

How can you convince them that this topic is worth bothering with?

DOI: 10.4324/9781003440826-77

Avoid saying

"Well, this topic could be useful if you ever needed to do X."

Reframe for success

"We don't always study things because they're useful; we also study things because they help us see the world in a different way."

Why does this work?

Students often have a very functional view of education. They tend to value things that bring immediate enjoyment or things that have an obvious practical application in "the real world." And, in a society that increasingly prioritises academic endeavours that seem to guarantee a route to high earnings, who can blame them?

But when we start trying to justify elements of subjects in this way, we reinforce utilitarian views of education, where everything must have relevance to society at large to be deemed worthwhile. By challenging this dominant worldview, we advocate for things that might seem superfluous but end up fascinating students. Complex problems to be solved, beautiful objects to be admired, ideas about the human condition to be considered. This kind of approach can liberate students, helping them to understand that learning seemingly unimportant things can be deeply rewarding in itself.

Next steps

1. **Display your passion for obscure knowledge** – Hook them in by telling stories about your strange specialisms. With plenty of passion, those quirky things that you love start to interest them too.

2. **Talk about things that you learned to enjoy** – Use anecdotes about things that you initially found boring about the subject and talk about what changed your mind about these topics.

3. **Discuss less obvious benefits of learning** – Certain things you ask them to learn might have little practical purpose. But talk to them about the other qualities they instil. Things like thoughtfulness, empathy and personal expression.

The class that's unsettled by social time issues (#76)

The scenario

Everything is set up for a successful, productive lesson. Resources are laid out neatly on the desk. Instructions are delineated clearly on the board. The classroom is a haven of tranquillity, awaiting the arrival of happy, enthusiastic students. All is serene.

As the bell goes, however, a cacophony of voices fills the corridor. Gossip. Arguments. Complaints of injustice and threats of reprisals. It's all kicked off during social time; circumstance has ruined your plans for an orderly and seamless lesson opening. All is chaos.

How can you possibly get your lesson back on track?

DOI: 10.4324/9781003440826-78

Avoid saying

"I don't care what happened at break. I don't want to hear another word about it!"

Reframe for success

"I appreciate that something unsettling happened at break. Have 30 seconds, take a deep breath and settle yourself before we begin."

Why does this work?

By acknowledging that some students are upset by events that took place before your lesson, you go some way towards recognising their feelings of hurt and frustration. Refusing to concede that there might be some legitimate reasons for excitement, and anger can deepen their sense of unease and resentment.

Giving time for everyone to calm themselves is vital. If the incident was particularly serious, you might need to extend the settling down time to a couple of minutes. You might even allow students to put their heads on the desk for this short period of quiet. Making it clear that work will begin soon – and that now isn't the time or place for an inquest into the events – illustrates that learning is the priority but that you empathise with their feelings.

Next steps

1. **Maintain a calm atmosphere –** You might need to rethink your starter and get them doing something that can be achieved independently. Keep things calm through silent reading, straightforward written questions or simple problems to solve.
2. **Avoid questioning irate students –** Some students take longer to deal with feelings of aggrievement. While they process their anger, let them quietly get on with work. Instead of asking them work-related questions in this class, ensure you call on them during the next lesson.
3. **Look out for patterns –**It might be that things tend to flare up at certain points of the week. Find out if something happens during these social times and request a pastoral or SLT presence as you manage these transitions.

The student who says they're rubbish at the subject (#77)

The scenario

This is their Achilles' Heel. This is the chink in their armour. This is their soft underbelly. Their soft spot. Their fatal flaw. Their nemesis. Whichever clichéd idiom about weakness we reach for, one thing is certain: they think they're crap at this topic. Whether it's coding, coordinates or catching a ball, they have decided they can't do it.

It's reached the stage where this mindset is now as immovable as a mountain; they have a fixed, seemingly permanent, belief that not only are they rubbish at spelling or sketching or public speaking, they will *never* be any good at it. Unsurprisingly, this perception is sapping their already depleted motivation levels.

Is there a way you can help them alter this self-defeating attitude?

 DOI: 10.4324/9781003440826-79

Avoid saying	Reframe for success
"Oh well, we can't all be good at everything."	"You might think that now but keep working on the feedback I've given you and you'll surprise yourself in the long run."

Why does this work?

If students get the sense that we also think they're rubbish at a subject, then the chances of them making much improvement are minimal. If their withering self-assessment of their abilities is not challenged it will create a negative self-fulfilling prophecy, leading to a vicious cycle of reduced effort, lower confidence and diminishing returns.

To counter this damaging tailspin, we must take every opportunity to tackle students' beliefs about an inability to succeed at a particular thing. Whatever that thing is, with skilful instruction, helpful feedback and lots of deliberate practice there's no reason why they can't get better at it over time. They might not be the next Marie Curie or Simon Schama but with a bit of perseverance they can certainly improve their knowledge of science or history.

Next steps

1. **Highlight specific areas for improvement –** Students tend to make sweeping statements like "I'm rubbish at maths." By helping them identify precise weaknesses, they'll see that there are concrete steps they can take to improve.
2. **Show them how far they've come –** Provide evidence of the progress they've made in aspects of a topic. They say they can't write introductions, so illustrate how these opening paragraphs have developed over the last couple of months.
3. **Give examples of how you improved –** Unconfident students will see your level of expertise as completely beyond reach, as though you were born with a golden gift for the subject. To counter this fixed viewpoint, reveal how hard you've had to work at some things and be open about which areas you still find difficult.

The student who makes a dramatic exit when asked to leave (#78)

The scenario

Following sensible application of the school's behaviour policy, you have no option but to ask a student to leave the room. To say the least, they are reluctant to go. Eventually, they get up and start to move towards the door. There's no chance, however, that they're going to go quietly. A nervous silence descends for a moment while the class waits to see what will happen next.

On the way out, they create a scene. An exercise book thrown on the floor. A muttered insult, questioning your intelligence. A slammed door as they exit the classroom.

How should you deal with this final, tumultuous act of defiance?

DOI: 10.4324/9781003440826-80

Avoid saying

"How dare you slam my door! You're in even more trouble now!"

Reframe for success

"Thanks everyone for continuing to focus on what we're doing. Let's keep working."

Why does this work?

There are a couple of explanations for why a student might behave in this way. First, they have lost their temper and are driven by a sense of unfairness at being asked to leave the lesson. Second, as they're going anyway, they've decided to create one last disruption on their way out, to provoke a response from you.

Either way, reacting to their exit will only add to the disruption. Unless there is the risk of someone getting hurt, ignoring their exit is the most effective approach. The class will be looking to see how you respond to the outburst; for some students a dramatic scene will provide a welcome distraction from their work, for others it will act as another unwanted interruption. By staying cool, and showing no outward reaction, you're modelling calmness and making it clear that continuing to teach the rest of the class is the priority.

Next steps

1. **Compose yourself** – Appearing unflustered, you've dealt with a stressful situation. But you'll probably have an increased heart rate. So, take the opportunity to stand at the back of the room and settle yourself with a few deep calming breaths.

2. **Beware scattergun warnings** – Other students might feel aggrieved at one of their peers being sent from the room. Avoid falling into the trap of immediately firing off rapid, multiple warnings at any students who complain.

3. **Reset the temperature** – If students continue to protest or disrupt, remind the class as a whole about your behaviour expectations, explaining that you will be happy to explain these again at break time if students would like to return to your room.

The class that won't settle (#79)

The scenario

As soon as they enter the room, noise levels rocket. There's an accompanying chaos of movement. Taking too long to get to their seats. Bumping into each other. Slamming bags on desks. A multitude of conversations desperate to be heard above competing chats.

Do now tasks are treated as we'll do it when we're finally ready tasks. You remonstrate with them, and they eventually settle. But it's tiring and frustrating. Why does every lesson have to begin like this?

What should you do differently?

DOI: 10.4324/9781003440826-81

Avoid saying

"You should have your books open by now. I shouldn't need to remind you to get on with your work!"

Reframe for success

"Thanks to those who already have their books open … Now I can see more of you getting started too."

Why does this work?

It's natural to feel frustrated when a class just won't settle. But voicing these frustrations at the start of a lesson creates a negative atmosphere. It seems like the teacher is on their back from the outset. Rather than coaxing students along, it appears that the teacher is merely fed up with them and is nagging them again.

By contrast, narrating the positives positions the teacher as someone who sees the best in children. This technique recognises the individuals that are doing what is expected, rather than subjecting them to the same criticism as the ones who aren't settled. Yet, with great subtlety, it also encourages those that aren't doing the right thing to follow the compliant crowd.

Next steps

1. **Meet them at the door** – One way to minimise disruption at the start of a lesson is to greet them at the door, very briefly explaining your expectations: "Open your books. Task on the board."
2. **Reinforce with gestures** – You may get to the stage where just a few students aren't responding to positive narration. If this occurs, give them a non-verbal signal to indicate that they need to open their books (#89) and begin writing (#90).
3. **Justify your routines** – Children are more likely to follow instructions if they understand why they are given: "we complete our do now tasks individually, in silence and without notes, so you get the full benefit of retrieval practice".

The class that keeps using their mobile phone in lessons (#80)

The scenario

At most points during any given lesson, you feel like you're only really ever talking to about 80% of the class. Whether you're explaining, questioning, giving instructions or students are working independently, there's a constant sense that you're never getting the full attention of the class.

The tell-tale signs are always there: the insistent ping of an incoming text; the furtive glance below the desk; the subtle whispers and smirks, as a message gradually spreads its way around the room. Teaching is hard enough as it is without competing with this ubiquitous device.

How can you get them to leave their phones alone?

DOI: 10.4324/9781003440826-82

Avoid saying	Reframe for success
"Can you please just put your phones away!"	"I haven't given permission for phones to be used. I'd prefer not to, but I will confiscate them if necessary."

Why does this work?

Teaching in schools where mobile phones are banned in lessons is much easier than in schools with vague rules about acceptable usage. If you're unfortunate enough to have to manage the use of these highly addictive devices in your classroom, the best bet is to routinely prohibit their use and deal with infringements in the same way as any other act of defiance.

While you may get unfavourable comparisons to teachers who adopt a laissez faire attitude towards phones, you'll soon see the learning benefits. Giving students frequent reminders that you don't expect to see or hear phones sets out a very clear expectation. Immediately taking phones that are visible or audible reinforces that you won't accept them in your class.

Next steps

1. **Lobby for a ban –** You'll no doubt have to call for SLT support when some students refuse to hand over their phones. Use follow-up conversations with senior colleagues as a chance to press for a total ban, enlisting colleagues to do likewise.
2. **Explain why they hinder learning –** Research consistently highlights the significant negative impact the mere presence of a phone can have on student concentration. Help students understand how having phones nearby disrupts their focus and model this by ignoring your own phone in class!
3. **Take pre-emptive action –** Between lessons, have quiet conversations with students who have difficulty ignoring their phone. Encourage them to put their devices inside your desk for the duration of the lesson. Ask for pastoral support to achieve this with reluctant students.

PART B
You say it best when you say nothing at all

Stop talking (#81)

The scenario

The children in the class go chatter chatter chatter. And yappity yappity yap. And blah blah blah. In place of an atmosphere conducive to productive work, there's a miasma of noise hanging in the air. Snippets of conversations – about birthday parties, social media celebs and who was mean to whom at break time – reveal the trivial, off-task nature of the chat.

Your attempts to tamp down this invasive gossip have proven ineffective. You ask them to be quiet at least five times per lesson but periods of lasting quiet are few. The only time you can get consistent calm is during a test, when they maintain the silence for the duration of the assessment. But otherwise, with this cacophonous class, noise reigns.

How can you stop them from talking constantly?

DOI: 10.4324/9781003440826-84

Avoid saying

"Shush!"

Non-verbal signal for success

Why does this work?

It might resemble the white noise intended to comfort a newborn to sleep, but "shushing" will not pacify older children for long. Shushers tend to fall into two camps. The first group tolerate deafening noise levels until they snap, before emitting a shush of such ferocity that it sounds like the sudden release of air from a bouncy castle. The second group shush almost constantly, punctuating every other word with the persistent hiss of an irate cobra.

In the first case the intense shush brings brief respite before students return to high volume. In the second case the shushing is viewed as background noise, like the steady but persistent buzz of the ceiling strip lights. As such, it is routinely ignored. By contrast, a finger over the lips signals a need for silence in a non-intrusive, non-threatening way that carefully targets individuals rather than frustrating the whole class.

When should I use it?

1. **When waiting for a few students to stop talking** – A finger to the lips is an ideal replacement for "stop talking and listen to me." It's universally understood and leaves straggling chatters no room for ambiguity about acceptable noise levels.
2. **During question and answer sessions** – Students often try to instigate conversations while other students are responding to your questions. Scanning the room and giving the signal to any students attempting to chat helps prevent disrespectful talking.
3. **To avoid being interrupted when you're talking or reading** – Being talked over by students can be infuriating. It's enough to make you break your flow and lambast the culprits. It's far better, however, to take a momentary pause and give them the clear finger to lips signal, indicating they need to cease their chat immediately.

Look at the board (#82)

The scenario

No two classrooms are the same. Even in schools where the classroom layout is designed to be uniform, the individuality of the space takes over. But despite the differences in layout, nearly all classrooms share one central design feature: a board at the front. It may be the latest interactive touch screen, or it may be a tatty whiteboard, devoid of sheen. Either way, regardless of the subject being taught, you will want students to be looking at it frequently.

Getting your students to pay full attention to the contents of your board, however, is proving difficult. Vital diagrams, key vocabulary and important notes don't receive the necessary attention. As a result, you're spending far too much time telling students to look to the front and concentrate on the essential knowledge that the board contains.

What can be done to keep them focusing on the board?

DOI: 10.4324/9781003440826-85

Avoid saying

"[Student's name], stop daydreaming and look at the board."

Non-verbal signal for success

Why does this work?

Ever sat through a presentation and found your attention wandering in and out? As an adult, you probably find it easier to regulate yourself and renew your concentration after periods of drift. The relationship between adults and other adults, and teachers and students is different, of course. But the point still stands. Publicly berating them for natural attention lapses is unlikely to motivate them to improve their concentration levels.

Instead, nudge students back to full focus through a non-verbal sign to regain concentration and pay full attention to the key information on the board. By jerking your thumb repeatedly backwards, like an optimistic hitchhiker on the slip road of a busy motorway, you can signal that they should be directing their eyes to the board behind you. Crucially, this motion removes the belligerent tone and sense of targeting students who have drifted off.

When should I use it?

1. **When individual students aren't paying attention** – A thumb behind you gives an inaudible reminder to focus. Best accompanied with an initial encouraging look, it can be ramped up to a stare (#98) if you're becoming frustrated by their poor focus.
2. **After a turn-around signal (#93)** – The combination of rotated finger then hitcher's thumb signals neatly that they need to spin back round *and* look closely at the board.
3. **When drawing the class's attention to a key point** – Gestures can also be very useful as part of everyday explanations. If you're making an important point, a backward thumb or tap (#92) on the board can both encourage them to direct their attention and place emphasis on the significance of this piece of information.

Listen to me (#83)

The scenario

Unbeknown to you, in the lesson so far the student has done the following. They've read a laminated health and safety information leaflet, which was Blu-tacked to the wall circa 2004. They've counted the number of damaged or discoloured ceiling tiles (23, if you really want to know). They've watched a fly make repeated efforts to penetrate a closed window.

Later, they've cleaned under their fingernails with a biro lid. Then they've spent time pondering whether to order the cheese and tomato panini or the chicken nuggets for lunch, when, suddenly, you've spotted them and got annoyed that, yet again, they weren't listening to a word you were saying. And they wonder why they struggle with the work!

How can you get them to pay attention to what you're saying?

DOI: 10.4324/9781003440826-86

Avoid saying

"You need to start listening, [student's name]."

Non-verbal signal for success

Why does this work?

At an individual level, repeatedly telling students to listen causes frequent interruptions to learning. By breaking the flow of teacher talk it risks leaving other students confused and frustrated. In classes where several students are regular non-listeners you can multiply these issues accordingly. Over time, teachers become angrier about having to give the same instructions again, and the atmosphere can become tense and hostile.

Through the simple wiggle of an earlobe, however, students can be reminded about the need to pay attention to what's being said in a non-confrontational way. Perhaps more importantly, the shaken earlobe gesture swiftly conveys the need to listen without adding to the cognitive load of students who are paying attention. Better still, the signal can be directed at different students without highlighting the accumulating poor focus.

When should I use it?

1. **During explanations –** There's nothing more infuriating for a class than meaning being lost while a teacher is explaining a complex concept. Prevent this from happening by signalling to unfocused students while you're speaking.

2. **If focus is lost while students are giving answers –** Similarly, avoid interrupting students responding to your questions. Do this by giving subtle signals to unfocused students while simultaneously listening to the person answering the question.

3. **When students drift off in assembly –** Admonishing a student during assembly can be off-putting for the speaker and creates a scene that can distract students' attention away from the key messages. A subtle ear-yank, accompanied by a glare (#98) is an ideal way to silence an inaccessible student seated in the middle of a row.

Don't do what you're about to do (#84)

The scenario

10-4, this is Charlie-Foxtrot over. Special observation update. I have eyes on the suspect over. I can confirm that the target is acting suspiciously, rummaging through a large black holdhall and pulling out what appears to be a bottle of transparent liquid. Suspect is now turning around and is preparing to use the weapon. Code red, code red. Back up required!

Teachers are not police officers, of course. And our students aren't criminals. No matter how much they might irritate us on occasion, we're not allowed to have them taken for interrogation by the FBI. But, at times, keeping a close eye on a class can feel like being on a stakeout, scanning the room for any sign of misdemeanours, actual or planned.

So, what should you do when spotting a student about to do something wrong?

DOI: 10.4324/9781003440826-87

Avoid saying

"Don't even think about doing that!"

Non-verbal signal for success

Why does this work?

Behaviour management is often reactive in nature. A student does something wrong, and a rebuke is given. A rule is broken, and a sanction is issued. A fight breaks out, and an investigation into what caused it begins. Even when the teacher spots the potential infringement in advance, chaos can ensue if it's not snuffed out quickly and discreetly. Shouting at the student interrupts the class and can encourage the student to carry on misbehaving. After all, they've already been told off. They might as well do the act, at least.

A proactive approach, however, can be used to prevent problems. Teachers tend to gain a sixth sense about poor behaviour issues *before* they occur. By slowly shaking our head from side to side, accompanied by a look of intense disappointment, we are signalling that the intended behaviour is unacceptable. But we're also helping students modify their behaviour. Over time they start to become grateful for our help in keeping them out of trouble.

When should I use it?

1. **When a student is messing with another's things** – In an attempt to wind up their peers, some students like to interfere with others' stuff. If you see them going to grab a lunchbox or highlighter, stop them short by giving them the sign.

2. **If a student is about to throw something** – Some classes (#27) like to launch items, often looking round first to see if they're being watched. With the head shake signal, their bent elbow can be frozen suddenly, so the object remains unthrown.

3. **During a test** – Students can struggle to maintain focus in an assessment. As you invigilate, the "don't do that" gesture is an invaluable tool to put an immediate end to a student's plans to talk, turn around or glance at someone's paper.

Stop doing that now (#85)

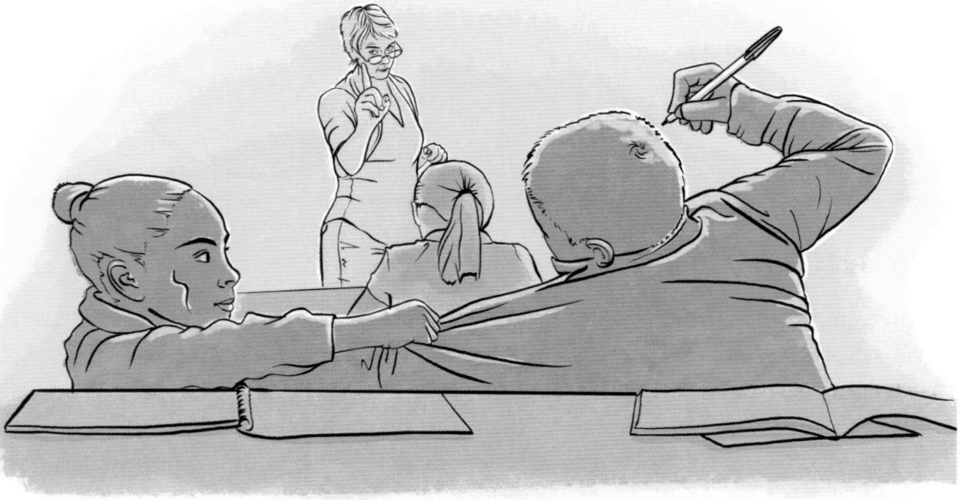

The scenario

At its best, behaviour management is proactive. The vigilant teacher spots potential issues and stops them happening. Ideally, a non-verbal (#84) will snuff out the flames of poor behaviour before they become an unstoppable inferno. But while our lighthouse beam arcs constantly, we can't always prevent the good ship behaviour from crashing into rocks.

Today, for instance, you spotted the following too late. One student drew a scar of blue ink along another student's cheek. A different student leaned out of the open window. A third student hid their friend's hockey stick as a joke. Each time, you spotted the offence but were too late to stop it happening. Each time, you were very irritated by the silly behaviour.

When catching students in the act, what should you do next?

DOI: 10.4324/9781003440826-88

Avoid saying

"What on earth do you think you're doing?"

Non-verbal signal for success

Why does this work?

Asking young people why they did something stupid is often futile. They usually don't know. It was for a laugh. Or they were retaliating. Or more likely, they weren't thinking at all. The irrational side of their brain thought it would be a good idea. By sounding vexed when tackling the poor behaviour you're more likely to create a scene than end the silliness.

A far less intrusive way to show your displeasure, and to get a student to stop doing something daft, is to silently wag your extended index finger from side to side. When supplemented with a stern look (#98 if really annoyed), it conveys the unacceptable nature of the behaviour without interrupting the rest of the class or antagonising the student. It may well be that you wish to sanction the student for the incident. But any necessary consequences can come later, without a most diverting drama for the class to enjoy.

When should I use it?

1. **When you catch them mid-act –** The index finger as windscreen wiper movement is ideal for silent reprimands of students caught with their hand in the proverbial cookie jar. Invariably, on receiving the signal they will immediately stop misbehaving.
2. **For less accessible students –** Certain classroom layouts make it very difficult to have quiet but firm words with students. Those at the end of a row, tucked away near the window, can be dealt with through this gesture rather than a verbal castigation.
3. **If you spot poor behaviour on duty –** Save your voice by not having to screech across the playground when you see a student being inappropriate. By catching their eye you'll be able to give them a calm and controlled signal instead. Crucially, you'll avoid the possibility of a heated discussion in the middle of a potentially large crowd.

Sit down (#86)

The scenario

Turning the handle repeatedly, so that it cranks to full power, you hear the familiar melody:

> Half a pound of chair superglue. Buying it was prudent. That's the way money goes. Pop! Goes the student.
>
> Round and round the classroom. Standing so impudent. They rise and rise, having fun. Pop! Goes the student.
>
> Up and down the classroom aisles. Playing mental truant. Round the room and back again. Pop! Goes the student!

How can you get this Jack-in-a-box to stay in their chair?

DOI: 10.4324/9781003440826-89

Avoid saying

"Sit down. Sit down! SIT DOWN!"

Non-verbal signal for success

Why does this work?

It's a truth not often recognised that stern imperatives quickly lose their power with regular use. When a teacher repeatedly commands a student to "sit down" or "stop talking" or "keep off the grass" or "leave me alone for ten minutes while I go and have a cry," the power of the authoritarian statement is rapidly diluted. What's more, it adds to the hubbub and disorder caused by students being out of their seats in the first place.

Through this magical movement, however, you can demonstrate telekinetic powers. A single finger raised up and down miraculously places a child in their seat, like a puppet on a string. It's amazing how students who display routine ignorance to a barked order to take a seat will comply in an instant to a non-verbal request. The depersonalised nature of the wordless signal creates an absence of confrontation. Do this and Jack will retire to his box pronto.

When should I use it?

1. **At the start of lessons –** Certain students like to use the entrance to class as an opportunity for a bit of "networking." You'll find you can cease their efforts to work the room by placing them straight in their seat with your supernatural finger.

2. **After lesson transitions –** At times, you'll need to ask students to move to a different activity or you'll want them to return to their seats after a practical task. In these circumstances, the paranormal digit will help them find their chair more speedily.

3. **For those about to wander –** Sometimes, students will want to leave their seat and approach your desk. That might be fine on occasion. If you'd prefer they didn't, however, give a swift signal for them to plonk back down before they fully rise.

Settle down (#87)

The scenario

You can hear the rumble of distant mayhem long before it reaches your door. Is it a horde of Viking raiders, marauding through the corridors in search of precious plunder? Is it the survivors of a nuclear apocalypse, charging through the canteen in their hunt for a charred cockroach to devour? Or is it the mud-splattered first XV rugby scrum, somehow diverted from the sports field, driving forward menacingly and trampling everything in its path?

No, it is none of these invading mobs. As they move to the end of the corridor on which your classroom is situated, you recognise some familiar faces. It isn't an army, it's just the class you'll be teaching in a minute or so. And they've arrived in a manner best described as wild and unruly, an alarming group full of thunderous noise and intense physicality.

How are you meant to even begin teaching this wild bunch?

DOI: 10.4324/9781003440826-90

Avoid saying

"You lot aren't coming into my room until you settle down!"

Non-verbal signal for success

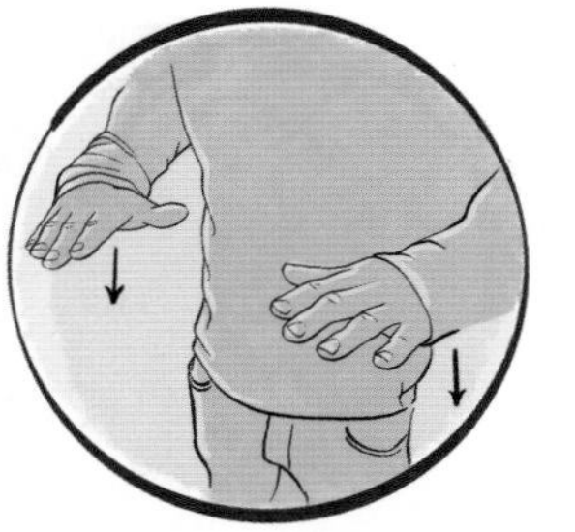

Why does this work?

When confronted with a disorderly crowd of students, it's tempting to try and stun them into silence. Screaming ultimatums at full volume outlining Draconian punishments will sometimes quieten a mob. But once it loses its shock value, students will ignore repeated shrieks. Whole-class threats tend to fail for similar reasons. Some students will be delighted to waste learning time by practising queuing or entering the room quietly for ten minutes.

Far more useful is a wordless gesture that tells them to settle down immediately without the need for any confrontational stand-offs. Moving a horizontal pair of hands slowly up and down signals soundlessly that the time for play is over. It reminds them that they are now entering a calm and disciplined domain in which loud noise and jostling are unwelcome. Once you've got them in the class, you can address the unacceptable corridor behaviour. Attempting to tackle it in the midst of the commotion usually provokes further bedlam.

When should I use it?

1. **When meeting and greeting on the corridor** – Standing at the doorway allows you to settle a wayward class before they step over the threshold. It gives you the chance to divert any non-settlers while calmer students get on with the do now.

2. **As students enter the class** – If you're unable to meet them outside the door, ensure you are near the entrance to gesture to any student whose behaviour is still too lively. Combined with a silent signal (#81), this should ensure a more serene start.

3. **With persistent latecomers** – Not all students enter your class at once. Giving noisy latecomers a settle down signal will help mitigate against further disruption.

Well done (#88)

The scenario

The road here has been difficult. You got off to a bad start. The opening fortnight was torturous, and the end of term run-in was grim. You'd rather not dwell on that week in mid-winter and the less said about that assembly in spring the better. But, after many months of struggle, you've managed to build a solid rapport with a "challenging" student. Now, they behave well and try their best in lessons. So, what could possibly be the problem?

Well, you want to show this student that you're pleased with their progress. You want to let them know you're impressed by their remarkable behavioural metamorphosis. But each time you praise them their behaviour worsens. It's as though they aren't programmed to accept praise. They view your positive comments as an affront to be resisted or ignored.

How can you show that you're proud of their efforts?

DOI: 10.4324/9781003440826-91

Avoid saying

"Good to see you finally working so well, [student's name]."

Non-verbal signal for success

Why does this work?

There are various reasons why some students don't like praise. First, they may find being singled out for special attention embarrassing. This is especially true of students who are unduly influenced by peer pressure and would rather their hard work slip by unnoticed. Second, students can see overpraise as condescending when they know they haven't really earned the plaudit. Perhaps they feel that your expectations of them could be higher?

A discreet thumbs up, by contrast, offers a visual reminder that they're on the right track. It avoids the use of patronising, empty superlatives, like wonderful, brilliant or awesome. Instead, it offers a brief shared moment which carries the simple message: carry on doing what you're doing. Crucially, it doesn't place them centre of the classroom stage; it can be deployed without any other students seeing it, which reduces social awkwardness.

When should I use it?

1. **To motivate students who dislike public praise** – Perfect for those who are worried about attracting the "swot" label, a subtle raised thumb acknowledges their efforts without drawing attention to their newfound compliance and conformity.

2. **When a correct answer is given** – Sometimes you want to spend time deconstructing why a response is right. At other times, only a cursory confirmation is needed. A quick thumbs up can let them know it's correct before moving on swiftly.

3. **As a prompt to start working** – When supplemented with a look of puzzlement, a thumbs up can be transformed into a sign that effectively asks, "do you understand? Is everything ok?" The answer is, invariably "yes," prompting them to get started.

You should be reading (#89)

The scenario

For a period of at least 230 million years, dinosaurs roamed the Earth. When we account for the fact that our most primitive … eh, what does "primitive mean"? … ancestors only appeared five to seven million years ago, that's an incredibly long time indeed.

But there is scientific agreement that about 66 million years ago … ooh, I'm getting hungry now. Do you think anybody heard my stomach rumbling? … a mass extinction event happened, where dinosaurs suddenly seem to have been wiped out. I wonder what's for lunch. I hope it's not pasta and tomato sauce again …

When they drift off during reading, how can you get them to concentrate on the text?

DOI: 10.4324/9781003440826-92

Avoid saying

"Open your book and start reading now."

Non-verbal signal for success

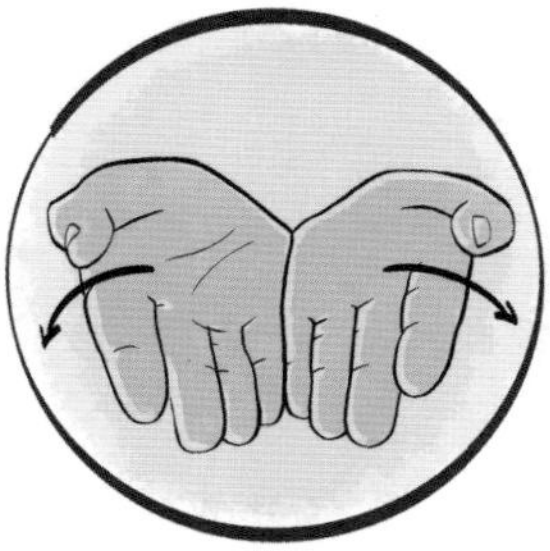

Why does this work?

Books stay unread for a variety of reasons. Students can lose focus and start thinking about other things. Or they might be intimidated by the level of challenge contained within the text. Or they might think that the topic is boring, and they'd rather look at something else. Whatever the cause, an irate instruction is less likely to motivate them to pick up the book in earnest. After all, reading can be a difficult and unappealing activity for some students.

While you can't allow students not to read their books, you can use less forceful methods to get them to open the book and follow along. Palms placed together, as if in horizontal prayer, then opened into a V shape, signal that it is now time to properly engage with the reading material. This subtle instruction offers a clear but encouraging signal that they must keep up with the text, even if they are bored with the topic or find the activity difficult.

When should I use it?

1. **If students aren't listening as you read** – Some students prefer just listening to the reader (you or another student) rather than reading along. But if you're sure this isn't the case then signal for them to open their books and start concentrating.

2. **As a reminder during silent reading** – Silent reading time equals mental truancy for some students. Tell-tale signs include reading the same book all year and "reading" upside down. Apply the open book gesture to get these students back to the page.

3. **To encourage students to get books out of folders or bags** – This versatile signal can also be used to soundlessly prompt students to get their books out and begin reading. Rather than repeating your instruction simply motion that it's reading time.

Start writing (#90)

The scenario

They are active, busy and engaged. For the opening minutes of the task, they've shown skilful dexterity. Building a tower, they've considered the forces of gravity, as they attempted to balance this skyscraper of felt pens. Then they demonstrated their creativity, covering sheets of paper with elaborate designs, using a multitude of colours and shapes.

Alas, their actual work remains untouched. Each section of the carefully constructed worksheet remains emptier than the shelves of a Soviet supermarket. The answer boxes reveal vast expanses of white wilderness, intact and pristine, like the first fall of Siberian snow. They are active, busy and engaged. Just not on the thing they're meant to be doing.

How can you get them to begin their written work?

DOI: 10.4324/9781003440826-93

Avoid saying	Non-verbal signal for success
"Pick up your pen and start writing!"	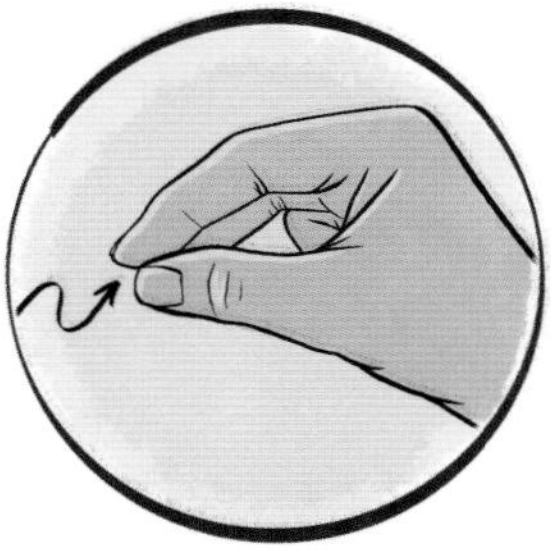

Why does this work?

For reluctant writers, the blank page can be an intimidating space. When students appear to be avoiding work out of idleness, there are often other reasons why they haven't begun writing. Their procrastination can be borne out of a belief that they aren't good at written communication. A stern command of the public variety is likely to add a sense of injustice to that feeling of inadequacy. They'll pick up the pen but will lack the motivation to keep going.

A less confrontational gesture, on the other hand, can give students an inaudible kickstart. Compared to the barked imperative, a mimed scribble across the palm signals that writing should commence but doesn't transmit the teacher's frustration in the same way. Wordlessly, it nudges them towards productivity without provoking the resentment of a spoken rebuke, enabling you to provide helpful feedback once they've written something.

When should I use it?

1. **With slow starters** – Students who take a while to get going gain particular benefit from the sideways scrawl gesture. Surveying the room from your desk, the signal can prompt any stragglers into written action without interrupting those who've begun.

2. **To nudge daydreamers** – Other students will drift off into contemplative states in the middle of a written activity. Leave 30 seconds to ensure they're not ruminating on spelling or vocabulary choice and then give them a sign to get back to their work.

3. **When working against the clock** – When moving towards timed responses ahead of an important assessment, certain students might need a reminder to speed up to avoid missing out vital sections of the paper. The zig zag scribble can help to get slower workers over the line as those last few precious minutes begin to evaporate.

I can see what you're doing (#91)

The scenario

Most students causing behaviour headaches can be spotted with relative ease. Without much thinking, they act up. They're bored so they start chatting openly to whoever's sitting next to them. They're meant to be talking about improper fractions, but they can be overheard discussing their favourite chocolate bar or what they did yesterday evening.

Whereas other students tend to be much trickier to notice. Before misbehaving, they undertake a swift reconnaissance, glancing furtively in all directions before tossing a rubber at someone's head. At other times, they'll undertake a quick check to see if anyone is looking before sneakily kicking a student's chair to make it seem like another student did it.

How can you let them know you're watching them closely?

DOI: 10.4324/9781003440826-94

Avoid saying

"I've got my eye on you, [student's name]."

Non-verbal signal for success

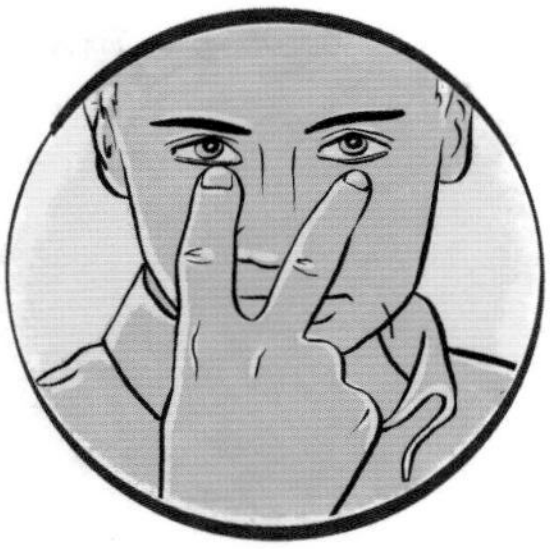

Why does this work?

Non-verbals work best when they aren't adversarial. Nearly all the non-verbal signals recommended in this section of the book are non-confrontational in nature. There's no doubt, however, that this gesture conveys the message that "I know you're up to no good and I'm going to be keeping an eye on you for a while." Before you reach the stage of serious mistrust, passive and conciliatory gestures – when students are about to misbehave (#84) or have been caught misbehaving (#85) – are much preferred.

Using this gesture, where two fingers to your eyes transition into a single digit pointed at the student, should therefore be seen as a last resort. It ought to be used only with students who routinely disrupt lessons in a sly and underhand way. It's regrettable that it needs to be employed at all, but it's certainly much better than losing your temper and announcing publicly that you're sick of a student and are going to be scrutinising their every move.

When should I use it?

1. **To let devious students know you're watching them** – Where deceitful students cause serial issues, a quick "I'm watching" signal can minimise the risk of further problems and let them know that you have them on your radar.
2. **When students are about to vandalise property** – Deliberate damage to school property is another context where niceties should be dispensed with. Use the eyes to stop a student who's about to draw over a desk or act dangerously with equipment.
3. **During detentions** – To avoid students being happy to return, detentions aren't meant to be too friendly. If students look like disrupting a detention, a finger to the eyes gesture can remind them that behaviour must be flawless in this setting.

Focus on your work (#92)

The scenario

Like a buff-tailed bumblebee, you circulate the classroom, pollinating knowledge as you go. Mimicking the busy winged insect, you buzz around from object to object, tireless in your aim to reach each one. Most targets welcome your arrival, offering smiles and gratitude in response to your guidance and feedback. All is tranquil in these sections of the garden of learning. Some targets, however, show stubborn resistance and remain hard to reach.

While you circulate, these students drift off into daydreams. Downing tools, they disturb others. They complete little work. Anything they do finish is rushed and substandard. Similarly, while you read from a text, or outline a problem to be solved, they ignore the work in front of them. Instead, they scan the room for more interesting distractions.

What's the best way to get them to focus on what's in front of them?

DOI: 10.4324/9781003440826-95

Avoid saying

"[Student's name], why aren't you working?"

Non-verbal signal for success

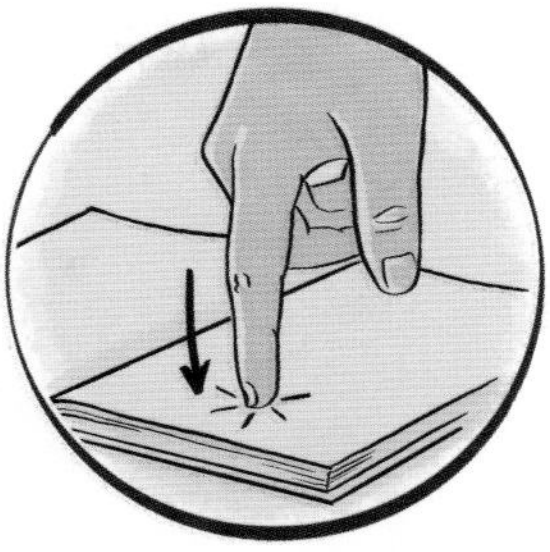

Why does this work?

Some teachers love rhetorical questions. *What do you think you're doing? When are you going to learn? Why do I bother?* When it's obvious a student is avoiding work, as opposed to being stuck and in need of support, asking "why aren't you working?" becomes a snarky criticism not a useful nudge. Generally, this criticism provokes an irritable response.

A non-verbal, by contrast, removes the truculent tone while still carrying the weight of firm expectation. Several brisk but authoritative taps on their exercise book makes it clear that you want them to concentrate on their work. But it does so without drawing the rest of the class's attention to them. It also allows you to assist other students nearby without interruption. Finally, it enables you to identify specific questions that need to be attempted.

When should I use it?

1. **During independent work –** You've given clear instructions and have modelled and scaffolded appropriately. But some students aren't keen to progress to the deliberate practice stage. Tapping on their work signals there is no excuse for any further delay.
2. **When reading aloud –** Students often take whole class reading as a chance for an unscheduled rest. By circulating as you read you can tap out morse code on their reading material, which translates as "keep up with what I'm reading."
3. **If they're facing the wrong way –** By tapping firmly on their work, you can get them to rotate quickly when they're surveying the room for possible distractions. Without having to give a verbal reprimand, you can make clear the need to regain focus.

Turn around (#93)

The scenario

Turn around. Turn around now. Turn around now, please. Turn around now, please, and get on with your work. Turn around now, please, and get on with your work otherwise I'm giving you a warning. Turn around. Turn around now. Turn around now, please. Turn around now, please, and get on with your work. Turn around now, please and get on with …

The student's rotations and owlish head movements are a constant disruption. In response, you've become riled and repetitive. Deeply repetitive. It's not just you who's become fed up with saying the same thing. The other students are becoming irked by the interruptions to their learning. So much time is taken up with trying to get the student to look the right way.

Is there a better way for you to get the student facing forwards?

DOI: 10.4324/9781003440826-96

Avoid saying

"[Student's name], I'm sick of seeing the back of your head!"

Non-verbal signal for success

Why does this work?

Over time, the power of a behaviour rebuke diminishes. Like black ink on a poster in direct sunlight, the message gradually fades. What starts as a powerful instruction becomes, through overuse, a background noise, comparable to the whirr of an overactive printer. By the time the frustrated teacher reaches the sarcasm stage, the relationship deteriorates, and the student ignores the instruction or twists back around only after a loud, begrudging sigh.

With a wordless signal, however, students are far less likely to be truculent and disobedient. A circular finger, like a calm and authoritative traffic cop, soon encourages the student to perform a swift U-turn and face in the correct direction. By removing the verbal element, the instruction becomes a non-confrontational, helpful visual reminder. As a result, they tend to comply quickly, without fuss, and without disrupting the other students.

When should I use it?

1. **During independent work** – There are few things more annoying than the silence of a hard-working class being punctured by a teacher telling one student to turn around. Instead, catch the student's eye and soundlessly direct them to spin round.

2. **While other students are speaking** – Berating students for facing behind disrupts the thinking of the rest of the class. By contrast, this gesture deals with the behaviour problem in an inconspicuous way, helping to maintain full attention.

3. **To get assistance from nearby students** – If turned around, students might not see your signal. Enlist help from nearby students by performing the gesture and nodding towards the backwards facing peer. The other student will then nudge them into looking your way, so that the signal can be repeated with their full attention.

Get a move on (#94)

The scenario

Tooth by tooth by tooth, the student gradually, almost imperceptibly, slides open the zip on the pencil case. Steadily, like a bomb disposal expert deliberating whether to snip the yellow, green or red wire, the student withdraws a writing implement from the cavernous recesses of the case. The pen – a dark navy gel instrument with a chewed and cracked lid – emerges. Slowly, oh so slowly, the lid is removed, displaying the nib's impatient glisten.

After a few minutes the student contemplates using the pen. Opening their exercise book, with the reverent delicacy of a white-gloved archivist handling a copy of the Guttenberg Bible, they eventually – after what seems like a period of hours – find their page. Slowly, oh so slowly, they underline the title three times and start drawing clouds around today's date …

How can you speed up this tortoise-paced student?

DOI: 10.4324/9781003440826-97

Avoid saying	Non-verbal signal for success
"Come on. Get a move on!"	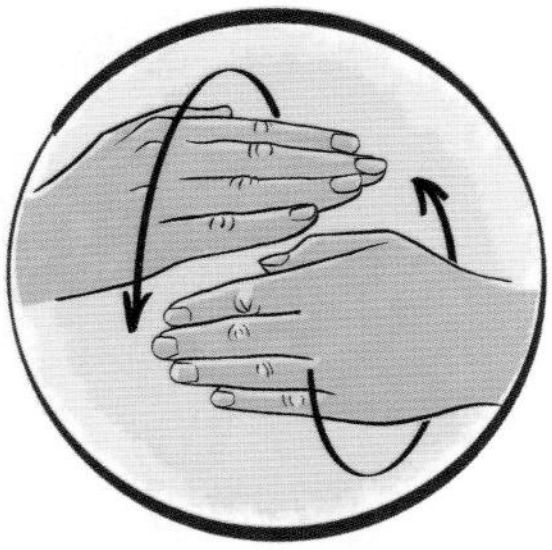

Why does this work?

On occasion, it's worthwhile making a statement of the obvious. Because sometimes, in the busy world of the classroom, we sometimes miss obvious truths. So here goes: students who are deliberately wasting time enjoy the opportunity to waste more time. All too often, a frustrated telling off provides them with that timewasting opportunity. It allows them to explain why they didn't get started or argue back that they weren't really wasting time or …

A silent hand gesture, minus the exasperated tone, is far more likely to chivvy along the most reluctant of starters. It provides a calm signal that immediate intellectual energy is required. A word of warning, though. Unlike most of the signals in this section, the rolling hands timewasting signal won't be universally understood by non-sport fans. As it's used by referees in sports like football, it will require pre-teaching to ensure all students understand.

When should I use it?

1. **With classic procrastinators –** Some students take aeons to perform very basic movements, like finding a page number or glueing in a sheet. Give them a sign that if they don't speed up, you'll be putting them in your referee's book!
2. **When students move very slowly around the classroom –** Simple tasks, such as sharpening a pencil or getting a textbook, can drag on interminably. Circling your hands makes it clear that you're putting them on the clock, and time is expiring fast.
3. **If you're dragging students in after break duty –** Legs can become suddenly weary once the bell has called them in for the end of social time. Save your voice and instead use the gesture to urge them along.

Develop your point further (#95)

The scenario

As classes go, this group of students are an odd bunch. Traditional behaviour issues – talking over the teacher, squabbling with one another, making immature comments – are non-existent. The class is quiet, eerily so at times. They could work in silence for hours. But when responding to your questions they are reticent to say more than a few words.

You've tried to nudge them along but with little success. You've increased wait time, rephrased and scaffolded the question, so it's easier to answer. But responses are still largely monosyllabic. Constantly urging students to "add more detail" or "develop your answer" is becoming tiresome for everyone; you're getting frustrated saying the same thing.

How can you get them to go into more detail?

DOI: 10.4324/9781003440826-98

Avoid saying

"Hmm. That answer is far too basic."

Non-verbal signal for success

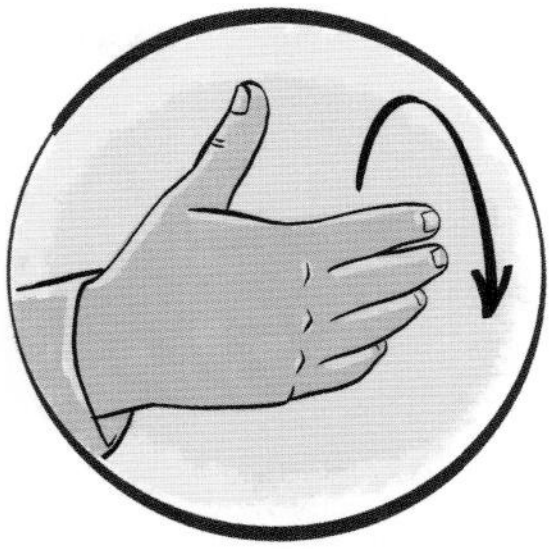

Why does this work?

There's no quick fix with a class like this. But displaying irritation at their reluctance to develop their points is counterproductive. Annoyance and blunt critique, in this context, will, in all likelihood, lead to fewer lengthy contributions rather than more. Repeating their shortcomings in a disappointed or exasperated tone will not encourage them to go deeper.

So, to remove the verbal awkwardness, it's helpful to use a signal to gently persuade them to expand on their thinking. And which signal does this? The wave: a vertical hand with a rotating twist of the wrist, which is reminiscent of Queen Elizabeth II's iconic greeting. Supplemented by an encouraging facial expression, complete with friendly nods, the hand asks them to go on, without the need for reminders that their answers are inadequate.

When should I use it?

1. **With individual students who make very brief contributions** – If students try to duck out after going into minimal depth, use the hand gesture to solicit more detail. Most students find it less intense than saying that they must develop their ideas.

2. **When students are unsure whether they're making a valid point** – Employ the gesture when students make a good point but become overcome with self-doubt. As they look pleadingly for reassurance, give them a sign that you'd love to hear more.

3. **During presentations when students get stuck** – Nervous students often freeze when giving a talk in front of the rest of the class. When they start to lose composure, give them a subtle roll of the wrist. This will help to persuade them that they are doing fine and that they should take a breath before continuing.

I'm waiting for silence (#96)

The scenario

With some classes, giving instructions and explaining things is simple. You talk and they listen. Or better still, you talk and they listen very carefully, giving their full attention, making notes of the really important things you say, even nodding along in recognition of the profound significance of the powerful knowledge you are in the process of imparting.

With some other classes, however, lengthy teacher talk is difficult. You'll be in the middle of delivering step-by-step instructions and have to pause to end a private chat between two students. Or you'll be explaining a complex idea when a student will put up their hand to ask an irrelevant question about arrangements for break time. Given the range of interruptions, you'll sometimes find yourself speeding up to try and beat the next inevitable stoppage.

DOI: 10.4324/9781003440826-99

Avoid saying

"I'm *still* waiting for you to stop talking!"

Non-verbal signal for success

Why does this work?

Giving a verbal reminder to the class that you're waiting for silence is helpful. But repeating that reminder with an exponentially irritated tone demonstrates to your students that you are becoming flustered and angry. While the anger may well be justified it will do little to discourage students from interrupting again. After a calm spoken reminder, it's far better to give a non-verbal signal that you're not prepared to wait much longer for silence.

Body language experts will tell you that one's arms across the chest is a sign of defensiveness and unease. But when used theatrically, with a disappointed tilt of the head and an occasional glance at the watch, this gesture conveys a different emotion. In this context, crossed arms suggest a controlled impatience and clear expectation that chatter must stop. It's helpful to stand elsewhere (e.g. the other side of the board, away from your desk) when you employ the gesture. This signals clearly that you have activated wait mode!

When should I use it?

1. **During explanation and instructions** – Give a brief reminder about not talking while you're talking, then fold your arms for any further stoppages. Students will recognise that this gesture, and your abrupt silence, means that their chats will have to cease.

2. **At the end of student discussion tasks** – Students can be reluctant to bring their discussions with other students to an end, especially if they are off-topic. Once you instruct them to stop talking, if they continue, move to folded arms after 30 seconds.

3. **When bringing writing tasks to an end** – Remind students to end their work with "pens down, stop talking, looking at me." Then employ the gesture if they linger. Other students will helpfully nudge them to let them know that you're still waiting.

I'd like you to answer my question (#97)

The scenario

Teachers use their voices a lot. Over a five-period day, they'll use thousands of words. Greeting and instructing and explaining and summarising and reminding and responding and cajoling and remonstrating and encouraging and congratulating and critiquing and clarifying and on and on and on. It's no surprise that it's not just our throats that become worn out.

Questioning is one area where you often feel like you use your voice unnecessarily. *Ahmed, what do you think? Josie, can you add to that? Do you agree, James? Is that correct, Li?* It sometimes feels like you're repeating the initial question for the sake of it and attaching a name for no good reason. Particularly when you've got to know the class really well.

Is there a way you can cut out wasteful words during questioning?

DOI: 10.4324/9781003440826-100

Avoid saying

"Erm…ok…who shall I ask next?"

Non-verbal signal for success

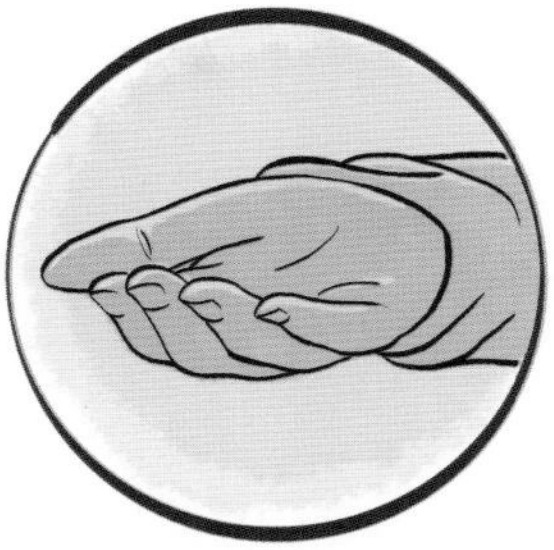

Why does this work?

Once you've established yourself with a class – and have displayed professional courtesy by learning their names quickly – seize opportunities to rest your voice and reduce the cognitive load caused by unnecessary questions. Scanning the room and pondering who to ask can also make you appear indecisive and make your questioning seem unplanned.

Instead, when the chance arises, change your hand from a fist to a horizontal flat palm, and point it in the direction of the student you would like to answer. As long as your eye contact is well-targeted, the student should have little problem realising that they have been asked to respond. This polite but confident gesture brings a seamless quality to your questioning.

When should I use it?

1. **When there's no ambiguity about who you'd like to answer** – If you're using hands-up questioning, and students volunteering to respond aren't seated nearby, this offers an ideal opportunity to soundlessly signal for them to answer the question.

2. **To go back and forth during discussions** – Debates and discussions provide a perfect chance to use this prompt. Through a simple movement from left palm to right palm, you can moderate an alternating debate or discussion in helpfully impartial silence.

3. **As a prompt for a student to begin talking** – As well as during questioning, the directed palm gesture works as an effective signal for a paused student to begin reading, to start talking again after an interruption or to launch into a presentation.

I'm really quite annoyed now (#98)

The scenario

After prolonged periods of overuse, your throat is shredded. Repeated straining has left you raw and hoarse. Fatigued and swollen, your vocal chords have finally given up, rendering you sore and voiceless as the end of term approaches. How did you get to this point?

The answer is simple: managing *that* class has destroyed your larynx. You start with a shush but the noise returns, consuming the classroom atmosphere after seconds of silence. A shush becomes "quiet now." A "quiet now" becomes "that's enough." A "that's enough" becomes a full-throated "BE QUIET." They settle down but the voice-blitzing cycle returns.

How can you show your annoyance without injuring your vocal chords?

DOI: 10.4324/9781003440826-101

Avoid saying

"Right, that's it. I've absolutely had enough of you!"

Non-verbal signal for success

Why does this work?

Being shouted at can put classes in a state of high alert. It leaves them waiting for the next fight or flight situation, meaning they are so focused on the volume of the shouting that they pay little attention to the words being screamed. It erodes trust and leaves teachers feeling stressed and on edge. It's bad for the mental health of teachers and students. Not only is yelling damaging to teacher/student relationships, however, it's also murder on a teacher's most important instrument: their voice. Without a voice, teaching is impossible.

Removing irritation, annoyance and anger from the teaching experience is also impossible. Even the mildest-mannered professionals feel vexed by student conduct at times. Initially, the trick is to disguise that annoyance through calm cues and neutral non-verbals, like a finger on the lips (#81) to signal for silence. Some classes, however, push beyond these amiable reminders. But even when inwardly furious, using Medusa-like stares rather than out-of-control howls helps maintain your equilibrium, while achieving more lasting results.

When should I use it?

1. **With students who've ignored gentle reminders –** When you're tired of repeating yourself, rather than yelling, lower your brow and give a steely stare. Amplified by the addition of a tilted head, this is often enough to avoid any further action.

2. **In response to some silly comments –** Some immature comments need to be addressed with strong words or sanctions. Other daft outbursts can be dealt with through a dismissive stare, which lets the student know how unimpressed you are.

3. **To silence those lacking focus in assembly –** If other adults are addressing a large audience of students, there is no room for tolerance of inattention, chatter or giggling. One intense look can help silence students located outside of reach.

Stop moving (#99)

The scenario

There's a spine-tingling feeling of anticipation here at the blue-ribbon event. The kind of drama that only an elite 100 metre race can generate. The line-up is breath-taking. Personal bests and bragging rights are up for grabs. And, of course, the medals that these athletes have been dreaming about through those long training sessions over the lonely winter.

And they're off! There's the suspicion of a false start but the roar of the crowd propels the participants forwards. Oh, it looks like we have a faller! One student has tripped up over a stray bag. They've faceplanted into a display about the water cycle! Undaunted, the leaders dash forward towards the finishing line. There's no ticker tape, just the open classroom door of a teacher preparing to greet a screaming, sprinting class for the start of the next lesson.

How can you possibly get this running mob ready for your class?

DOI: 10.4324/9781003440826-102

Avoid saying

"Oi! Don't take another step!"

Non-verbal signal for success

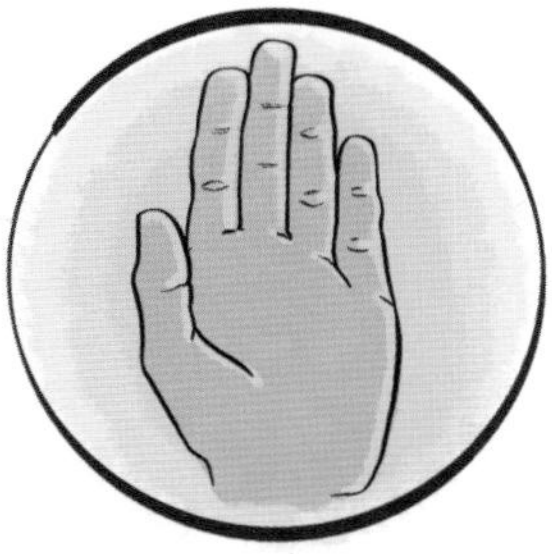

Why does this work?

When dealing with hyperactive and reckless behaviour, the natural inclination is to stretch our vocal chords to the maximum, in order to outdo the din of the herd. By wailing like a demented hound, the theory goes, you'll transform the rampaging horde into a silent, orderly, almost statuesque queue. In reality, the noise tends to amplify the levels of anarchy. It causes a further surge in students' adrenalin levels, leading to further chaos.

When their noise levels go high, yours should go low. A firm, unambiguous gesture pauses them without the need for banshee level wailing. Like a traffic cop halting a six-axle juggernaut, an upright palm, from an extended arm, stops students moving too quickly towards the classroom. Sanctions for wild behaviour can come later. For now, use this imposing but non-threatening gesture to settle them down before the lesson commences.

When should I use it?

1. **When students run on the corridor** – Ideally, you'll be at the door keeping an eye out for disorderly arrivals in the distance. A raised palm can decelerate their stomping feet, and calm them right down, before they get anywhere near your door.

2. **To calm students entering the room** – If you haven't managed to greet them as they come into view, the next best triage point is as they make their way into the classroom. Any rushers or jostlers can be paused mid-step with a commanding hand.

3. **If you wish to keep students away from your desk** – Some students like to wander your way to show you work or ask you questions. If you'd prefer to go to them, simply raise a palm to signal that they can stay in their seat and you'll be over soon.

Come here – I want a word (#100)

The scenario

They've done something stupid. And you have irrefutable, indisputable proof that they did it. It might have been vandalising the desk. It might have been dropping a dictionary out of the window. It might have been purposely kicking a younger student's ball over the fence.

Whatever it is that they've done, there's no doubt that it was a ridiculous, reckless act. Naturally, you're fuming. It was intentional, it was thoughtless, it was selfish and unkind. You feel like unleashing a verbal blitzkrieg upon them. You feel like releasing the full force of your fury, in front of their peers, so that they'll think twice before doing something like this again.

Is this the best approach?

DOI: 10.4324/9781003440826-103

Avoid saying

"Oi! [student's name], come here now!"

Non-verbal signal for success

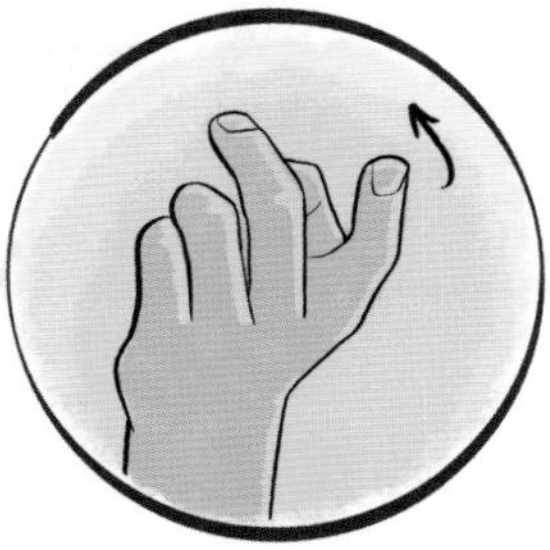

Why does this work?

Shouting at a misbehaving student can act as a vent for teacher anger. But it is likely to inflame the situation. Moreover, it serves to illustrate a loss of control on the teacher's part. Mindless behaviour might seem to warrant a public roasting. Yet even egregious offences are usually better dealt with calmly, away from the glare of peers. Unless student safety is at stake, raised voices merely exacerbate negative emotions and can cause lasting conflict.

A moving hooked finger, by contrast, conveys burning annoyance without needing a scary bellowing voice. Beckoning a student gives an unambiguous indication that you want an urgent word. It also helps nearby students recognise that you will be dealing with the issue authoritatively but in a measured way. The student's long walk over gives you the perfect opportunity to take a deep breath, maintain calm and consider your next words.

When should I use it?

1. **In a busy canteen or playground –** Ideal for crowded environments, the "come to me" gesture enables you to deal with the aftermath of an incident away from rubbernecking students. If you scream, the room falls silent. But if you gesture, there's a far higher chance you can deal with the incident quietly and stay in control.

2. **Asking a student to step outside –** Tell a student to "get out" and it's harder to reintroduce them after a warning. A signal from near the doorway, however, enables a low-key return for the student once you've had an appropriate firm word outside.

3. **To have a discreet chat at your desk –** With a minor adaptation, the "come here" gesture doesn't always need to be used for tackling bad behaviour. A finger, waggled quickly, becomes a friendly sign that can be used to ask students to come to the front for any conversations that you don't want other students to be able to hear.

Index